D0064750

Myth of the
Entrepreneur

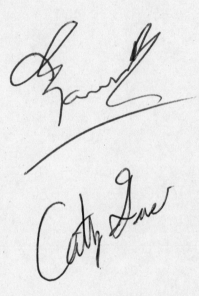

Myth of the Entrepreneur

A SEARCH FOR TRUE VALUE

Ravi Kailas

with

Cathy Guo

HarperCollins *Publishers* India

First published in India in 2019 by
HarperCollins *Publishers*
A-75, Sector 57, Noida, Uttar Pradesh 201301, India
www.harpercollins.co.in

2 4 6 8 10 9 7 5 3 1

P-ISBN: 978-93-5302-835-0
E-ISBN: 978-93-5302-836-7

Typeset in 11/15.7 Giovanni Book at
Manipal Digital Systems, Manipal

Printed and bound at
Thomson Press (India) Ltd.

For the family we have chosen
and the family we are yet to discover.

CONTENTS

FOREWORD

———◆———

THE earth may be a fact; but the world is an idea. Who authors this idea; how does our world come to be what it is?

A variety of forces – demographic, social, political, and historical – are all at play. That said, the drives and deeds of a rare breed of individuals are also major forces in shaping our world. We refer to that rare breed of individuals as 'entrepreneurs'.

What makes entrepreneurs, at least the successful ones, rare and influential? Simplifying, we can point to three reasons: one, their command of resources. Two, the power – not only economic but also social and political – that comes to accompany these resources. And three and perhaps most importantly, the unequal talent that is often at the root of their success and power.

Talent, it seems, is unequally distributed across humanity. What though of the distribution of the *fruits* of this unequal talent?

This question has long spawned doubt and not a little debate. Most recently, one may recall the former US president Barack Obama's provocative refrain to entrepreneurs, 'You didn't build that.'

In *Myth of the Entrepreneur*, Ravi Kailas, a successful serial entrepreneur (a member of the rarest of that rare breed), confides his confrontation with and contemplation on this question. His life journey is as gripping as it is unlikely. Marked by drama and serendipity, Ravi's journey leads us through a personal transformation from an individual entrepreneur to a collective value-creator, from striver to witness, from ego to the discovery of something new. For Ravi, the entrepreneur should not be just a clever arbitrageur or an ingenious creator, but also be a wilful trustee and caring agent of society.

In a world of worsening inequality, diminished trust in established social systems of rewards and tectonic shifts driven by technology and climate on the horizon, how can the entrepreneur refashion her worldview and responsibility to better create *and* distribute value for the world? In place of the conventional 'meritocracy' (the power of merit, where rewards go to the individual), can entrepreneurs realize and practise 'meritosophy' (the wisdom of merit, where rewards go to the collective good)? The point is not to abandon private enterprise or ownership, but to integrate it with broader ethical paradigms of value creation such as trusteeship.

———

When we speak of talent, we usually refer to the entrepreneur's competence – innate or learned. But if we are interested in understanding our world as an outcome that is influenced by entrepreneurs, competence is not the only factor to consider.

The world is not shaped by power alone, but by power *and* interests – understanding the distinction between the two is crucial. Power shapes the *quantity* of influence on social outcomes; while interests shape the *quality* of influence on social outcomes.

An entrepreneur's power is in his or her exceptional talent or competence. If leaders are regarded as merchants of hope, entrepreneurs are merchants of possibilities, of new frontiers.

But what about the entrepreneur's interests; what does the entrepreneur want? A conventional response is that entrepreneurs want the satisfaction of accomplishment, of 'winning'. And, understandably, also, 'making it big', attracting wealth and glory. If this is a bit of a caricature, it is the depiction of the entrepreneur that we most commonly observe.

In *Myth of the Entrepreneur*, a pang of conscience rouses Ravi to contemplate this convention. He finds beauty in and glorifies the talent and power of the entrepreneur. Yet he also finds a new possibility in the *soul* of the entrepreneur. His concept of an 'awakened entrepreneur' is a caring agent, whose principal is not *oneself* but society itself. The inspiration for this transformation in Ravi's thinking is deep and varied, and includes Vipassana meditation, the transmuted emperor Ashoka, the fabled entrepreneurs Jamsetji Tata and Chuck Feeney, and so on.

While competence may help the entrepreneur see what is 'true', it is character that can help the entrepreneur see what is 'good'. Just as the power of the entrepreneur should reflect merit, the interest of the entrepreneur should reflect wisdom. *Myth of the Entrepreneur* invites all talented entrepreneurs to reflect on the difference between power and interest, and how to understand the complex relations – and at times, contradictions – between the two.

The beauty of this book, and Ravi's story, is that it shines a spotlight not on the entrepreneur's competence but rather the entrepreneur's character. Competence is the cause of power; character is the cause of interests. It is via this moral reflection that *Myth of the Entrepreneur* links the talent and effort of the entrepreneur to the well-being of and solidarity with society and our world. Ravi invites entrepreneurs to aim for leadership in the market and trusteeship in society. It is in this manner that the book invites and challenges entrepreneurs to integrate (enterprise) performance and (societal) progress.

All said, Ravi's message and invitation here to entrepreneurs everywhere is at once timely and timeless. Note it well.

Prof. Subramanian Rangan
The Abu Dhabi Crown Prince Court Endowed Chair
in Societal Progress, INSEAD
Fountainbleau, January 2019

PREFACE

———◆———

As an entrepreneur, you learn to master serendipity. While determination, persistence, ingenuity and rationality are necessary ingredients for success, understanding how to seize the unexpected to your favour is essential. The labour, love and sheer serendipity that went into the book you now hold in your hands is nothing short of a miracle, not for the book's merits (which are still being determined), but for the unlikely set of events that brought the book into being.

I have spent a major part of my life preferring privacy, often deviating from my peers in industry and business who lead much more public-facing lives. When I first embarked on writing a book, it was with the intention of encapsulating some of the learnings and evidence I had gathered as an entrepreneur in India and as a citizen of the world – specifically the alarming trends in rising inequality, the attitudes and assumptions of wealth-creators, and the rising discontent towards the globalization-powered growth of the past two decades, which had enriched as many as it had left behind.

One question, above all, tormented and propelled me: what is the nature of *value*? What does it mean to value something – and how do we determine what is valuable – as an individual and as society?

I thought of myself as a relatively progressive and 'enlightened' fellow, who had found some insight into these questions and was implementing them in life and in business. But in writing this book, my assumptions and perspective have been broadened and challenged in ways that are revolutionary, and I am speaking as someone who has 'reinvented' his own mode of being many times over.

The book that you hold in your hands is the result of a collective effort. This effort was led by Cathy, whose brilliance and deep dedication not only brought the book into existence, but also opened my eyes to just how radical, powerful and humane the younger generation could be in reimagining the future. It was a deliberate choice of mine to put two voices together – one reflecting on the past and one looking towards the future. She assembled a brilliant team from multiple academic disciplines and backgrounds; together, we spent many evenings in my living room in London outlining, debating, reading, writing, discussing. Only 5 per cent of that research effort has landed in the final manuscript, but the learnings that we took from the process are lifelong.

It was also Cathy who suggested that we tell a personal story, rather than focus on theory. Although the implications of this made me uneasy, she (in true entrepreneurial fashion) converted our entire team of researchers, editors and publishers to (kindly) suggest the same until I conceded. From the heart attack at age thirty-eight, to the five years of meditation and wandering, to building the company of my dreams, these are some of my most personal and vulnerable memories as a human being, and I share them only with the thought that readers may take something for their own journey, or be more motivated to share their stories in turn.

Even after decades of searching, I have not hit on any final solution, and this book, above all, is a call to action for those like-minded individuals to join us, to allow us to help them, and to make their voices and stories known. I am certain after this experience that it is the younger generation who will lead this charge.

In the book, I write about the joy and honor of being a 'grain of sand' for many pearls, a small catalyst that disappears in the beauty of the final creation. This book is its own testament to that process – and I would not have it any other way.

Ravi Kailas
London, February 2019

ACKNOWLEDGEMENTS

To Cathy – for choosing to 'double down' at every fork in the road.

To Aiden, Yaniv, Joe, Zoey – for spending so many of your afternoons and evenings waxing philosophical in my living room.

To Krishan at HarperCollins – for supporting the spirit of the project from the very start.

To Suke from Oxford, Philip from Columbia, and most of all to Subi from INSEAD – for entertaining and encouraging the idea of a businessman attempting philosophy.

To Vikram, Daman and Aditi – for being the future I look forward to everyday.

And immensely, to the family who shaped and guided me – without whom there would be no story.

Thank you.

Part 1

DISPLACEMENT

Grasping at things can only yield one of two results:
Either the thing you are grasping at disappears, or you
disappear.
It is only a matter of which occurs first.

—S.N. Goenka

1

DESCENDING FROM THE PEAK

———————❈———————

DRIVE seventy minutes or so outside Mumbai's city centre and you reach the Sahyadri hills of the Western Ghats, the 'benevolent mountains' glittering in deep green, their peaks reaching into the mist-covered sky. It is a hiker's dream: multiple trails leading through the mountain passes, very few people, and a range of spectacular views, drops, cliffs, waterfalls and tributaries. There are only a handful of places in the world that can match the beauty of hiking in these mountain ranges.

It was March 2004, and I was hiking with two friends. We always started these hikes early in the morning so that we could return to the city before nightfall. By 11 a.m. we had already reached the peak of one hill and were starting to descend, walking carefully through the grassy trail leading to the next mountain.

'It's beautiful, beautiful beyond belief.' I said to my friend Nisha, who was busy taking photographs of the mountainside with her film camera, the lens opening and closing like a large, blinking eye. The midday sun was starting to creep up on us, shyly advancing before hemming us into its muggy heat. We hoped for rain – anything that would give us some momentary relief from the fierceness of the sun.

That's when I began to feel it. A tingling in my fingers. A growing ache in my chest and upper arms. Lightheadedness. Shortness of breath. All the classic symptoms of a heart attack.

In a shaky voice, I shouted to my friends that I needed to lie down.

They stopped and looked back at me while I wracked my mind for possible solutions, trying to keep my attention away from the dread that was descending on me like a heavy fog. We were in the middle of a long descent. Just to reach the base of the mountain would take an hour, and the nearest hospital was more than thirty minutes away from there. My driver would be asleep in the car, awaiting our descent. All I had was a Motorola flip phone with a non-existent signal. I could not reach anyone and I was unreachable.

My thoughts were like an unfinished jigsaw puzzle – rapidly assembled, jumbled and incomplete. It took every ounce of my remaining mental energy to accept that there was nothing I could do. I had to leave everything to fate.

With the help of my friends I lay down on a smooth black rock near the trail, thinking to myself that if I did not wake up, at least the last thing I saw would be the lush and serene foliage of the mountains I loved.

I was thirty-eight years old.

Two days later, I went to see a cardiologist in Mumbai. When I described to him what had happened, he recommended an immediate coronary angiography. The X-Ray images from the procedure confirmed my suspicion.

'You had a heart attack during the hike,' the doctor said, in an emotionless tone. 'Which is unsurprising, since one of your main arteries is clogged.' He paused so that I could take in each of these statements. 'I would say it is relatively serious.'

Doctors always use phrases like *relatively serious*, knowing that they mean little to the terrified patient. People either focus on *relatively*, or on *serious*.

'What do you mean by relatively serious?' I asked.

'Almost 80 per cent of your artery is blocked by hardened plaque.' He pointed to a dark spot on the scan of my heart. 'We recommend a coronary angioplasty as soon as possible.'

I chewed on the inside of my lip and stared at the scan unblinkingly. I was supposed to fly to Dubai the next morning for another round of investor meetings. Instead, I was doing the paperwork for removal of the built-up plaque in my heart.

'You know,' the doctor added, before leaving the room, 'the heart attack was what saved you. If you had waited a few weeks, your arteries would be so clogged that any heart failure would have likely been fatal.' The doctor then gave a faint smile and walked out into the hospital hallway.

I watched his white coat disappear into the crowd of patients waiting outside, a coloured sea of saris and kurtas, makeshift chairs and tin cans filled with homemade food delivered to the waiting patients by mothers and wives. So much of life lies in understanding scale; so much of India is the confrontation of it. In that moment, as one patient in Jaslok, a hospital in

Mumbai housing thousands of people, in a city of millions, I felt sheer powerlessness. The doctor's words were still ringing in my ears, but he had left me to process their implications alone.

The heart attack is what saved me, I kept thinking to myself. A warning flare signalling incoming disaster. What irony.

I will always remember that moment, sitting on the crinkled white sheet of the hospital bench, the shock cascading through my body like a chilled wave.

———

The hospital room in the intensive care unit at Jaslok Hospital was bare and functional. Huge doors opened into the room of fifteen beds, each separated by paper-thin dividers. There were no windows, no way for the eye to track the natural passage of time. It was a place of extreme silence, where even the slightest shuffle could be felt in the air.

I had been alone in the ICU for two days under close hospital surveillance after a procedure that removed the blockage of plaque from my heart.

'Don't worry,' I said on the phone to my mother, who still lived in Hyderabad, our home city in southern India, and to my wife, who was visiting family in a different part of the country at the time. 'The doctor said the procedure went well. Now they just need to observe me in recovery, to make sure there aren't any complications.'

'Is it serious? What exactly did the doctors say?' each asked in a panicky tone. I divulged as little detail as I could, knowing their tendency to worry.

'I will be fine. The doctor said I am in recovery now and should be discharged shortly,' I said, slightly smudging the truth. Given the size of the blockage in my heart, he had suggested many days of surveillance in the ICU. 'I think it would be best if I went through this alone. I will be home in just a few days.'

My family honoured my wishes; at this point they were used to my idiosyncrasies, a predilection for solitude being one of them. For the next week, besides a daily check-in from a great friend, Deepak, who lived close by, I was completely alone. The moments passed, painstakingly. I stared at the ceiling of the ICU, memorizing the cracks and patches of stains in the plaster. At night when I could not sleep, I could count each noise breaking the silence of the ward.

My 'real' life – that complex entanglement of people, routine, existing obligations – slowly retreated and fell away, leaving behind only the husk of my own consciousness and the silence of the hospital ward. When time and space were suspended in that way, you gained access to a mental space often drowned out by daily life.

Within that space, the familiar became strange. Time stalled altogether: the past was on trial, the future uncertain, and the present in limbo. It was precisely a process of denaturalization that struck me – all my assumptions about everything cracked, and were now open to interrogation. I did not know if I would survive, and whether, if I did, what my life would be like afterwards.

To this day I struggle to find words to precisely describe what I experienced in the Jaslok Hospital ICU that day. 'Revelation' as derived from the Latin, *revelare*, 'to lay bare', has a surgical quality to it that suggests a rational process, but I could barely make sense of the fragments of thought running through my mind. What I felt was indescribable. In fact, 'feeling' itself is not the right word, being far too rooted in the physical senses.

What I experienced that day was more akin to a shapeless intuition – all I knew was that whatever came out of those hours in the hospital would be a different life. I did not know how, or why. I could not come up with any rational or intellectual explanation. What I beheld in those moments was something powerful that I suddenly 'knew' but did not yet understand.

Days and nights passed in the ICU. I ran through in my mind the images and memories of the past few years. The same questions came up, again and again. How did I get here? Where was I going? What was the purpose of life, and why did I suddenly find this question so pressing and difficult to answer?

It had been eight years since I moved to Mumbai from Hyderabad, the city where I had lived all my life. In contrast to the lazy and residential Hyderabad, Mumbai had a distinctly frenzied tempo, and it was this energy that had originally drawn me to the city. Thousands of migrants streamed into Mumbai every single day, armed with dreams and ambitions, but also weighed down by fears and hardships. It was a city of constant change – always in flux, always in motion. A perfect place, I thought, to start a new life after leaving home.

Within a few years of moving to Mumbai, I was already actively running three of my own companies. I slept very little, often pacing up and down in my apartment until sunrise, lost in one frustrating analysis or another. I gained weight – slowly at first, then quickly. I used to joke about this, saying I wished everything about being an entrepreneur was as easy as the weight gain that seemed to come with the job.

Building companies and courting investors also demanded constant travel, which brought its own particular fatigue. I had logged more than 200 flights in the past year, travelling to New Delhi once a week, to Hyderabad every two weeks and to Hong Kong, Dubai, London or New York every month. One year, I was even granted the dubious award of Jet Airways' frequent flier of the year, which, looking back, seemed more like a warning than an accolade. My personal relationships, especially my marriage, strained beneath the obsessional energy I poured into my work.

Two years before my heart attack, I remember enjoying an evening of cocktails and hors d'oeuvres with Rohit Phansalkar. Ro represented a syndicate of major investors in my company; he was one of the first prominent Indian bankers on Wall Street, and would be a close associate throughout many of my future ventures.

'Ravi, you've been taking care of us – your investors – very well.' Ro had a signature voice, slow and gentle, which rarely revealed his real mood. He was a sophisticated man, naturally poised in a way that I could never pretend to be. He dabbed his mouth with a napkin in a regal manner.

'That's my job.' I replied. 'I'm happy that you're happy with the company's progress.'

Ro squinted his eyes, and I realized that his statement was leading up to something else. 'Yes, that is all well and good, Ravi. You have been taking care of *us*, but I do not think you have been taking care of *yourself*.' He sipped his drink and waited for my reaction.

Ro was a man who weighed his words carefully, and they struck a chord with me. In the span of a few years, I had turned from an idealistic graduate with dreams of making a mark in the world into an overworked, overweight entrepreneur who could allocate only fifteen minutes of his time at once. At the centre of it all was an inescapable emptiness, a doubt that reared its head in the solitary anguish of many sleepless nights.

More often than not, I suppressed that kernel of doubt, hiding it beneath activity after activity until, like a weak flame, it was snuffed out in the wind. We move through life with the assumption of having knowledge, but we know not what lurks within us.

———

For so much of my life, my role as an entrepreneur was the defining part of my identity. Even though the term 'entrepreneur' has taken centre stage in the public imagination in the twenty-first century, it is surprisingly difficult to define what exactly an entrepreneur *is*. Some define entrepreneurs as people who run businesses. Others categorize entrepreneurs as people who take on risk for potential profit, most commonly through some sort of business venture.

Still others believe that the definition of 'entrepreneur' should be expanded to include people who take on risk to develop products not necessarily just for profit, but also for other motives, such as social impact. Little did I know then that much of my life would be spent in trying to define this motive, not from the position of an entrepreneur but from that of a human being trying to make sense of life. What was the purpose of the activity to which I had dedicated so much of my time and effort? What was its ultimate aim or value? How did the value produced by or inherent to entrepreneurship relate to other values that I held? What was the relationship between wealth and value, and how could they be defined and distributed?

But I'm getting ahead of myself. These questions did not arise until much later. When I was younger and just setting out on my journey, my personal definition of entrepreneurship was built on my love for the process itself. Professor Howard Stevenson, the founder of entrepreneurship studies at Harvard Business School, defines entrepreneurship as 'the pursuit of opportunity beyond resources controlled'[1]. This resonated with me; entrepreneurship was *process* as opposed to product, means rather than ends. Entrepreneurship was a passionate 'pursuit' at its core, one that began with identifying opportunity, and ended with executing solutions. Profit was not the primary motive, but the standard by which inferior solutions could be filtered out from the competition. For a while I was preoccupied with this question of defining entrepreneurship, yet I could not seem to come up with any definition that satisfied me.

So, I was sitting with my drink one evening at the Belvedere Club in Mumbai with a few close friends when I posed the question. 'Just out of curiosity,' I asked, 'how would you define your profession, your jobs or roles in life?'

My table of friends fell silent (this was not the relaxed banter they were hoping for on a Saturday evening), until someone finally answered, 'Well, Ravi. I'm an artist. And I would say that an artist is someone who finds a space, enters it, and works.'

I was moved by the elegance of his response. Although it seemed simplistic, the definition captured the subtlest elements of artistic production.

To *find* a space required a constant alertness and sensitivity to inspiration, a kind of openness or porousness to the world. To *enter the space*, or to transform an inspiration into a defined structure that one was able to enter, required initiative, structure and innovation. Finally, to *work within the space* required diligence, persistence and fidelity to the original inspiration.

I was struck by how seamlessly the definition applied to entrepreneurship: locate the opportunity, structure the opportunity, and work to provide a solution within that structure. The definition resonated with a conviction that I always had about entrepreneurship – that it could be experienced, at its core, as an artistic pursuit. The opportunity was the canvas, and the solution was the painting. While it was desirable that the painting should gain fame or monetary reward, the most important incentive was one's love for the process of creation – the finding, the entering and the working – as a goal in itself.

I yearned to be such an entrepreneur, and I willingly sacrificed many aspects of my life for that singular goal. By the time I had the heart attack, it seemed that my dream had been achieved. Why was it, then, that no thought of any of the companies I had created crossed my mind in the face of death? Why were they not the core memories and achievements my mind retrieved when scanning the past? In my mind, I returned again and again to this contradiction, amidst the silence and insomnia of the ICU.

What I realized amidst the deafening silence of the emergency was that over the past few years, I had been unwilling to slow down or to assess my life from an external perspective. My focus was on endogenous elements – causes and effects within my existing system and routine. There was no real motivation to consider exogenous factors, to take a perspective from *outside* the system, beyond the life I had built. This created a blindness of sorts – an inability to question the assumptions and foundations on which my life was built.

To take a perspective from outside a system and question its functioning is an important exercise for anyone in any station of life. The Sanskrit term *samsara*, which could mean 'wandering', and also 'world', is meant to indicate that humans are born into an existence of cyclical drift – we wander into the world and through the world, often retracing the same paths unknowingly. Samsara serves as a warning, a reminder that we could each remain ceaseless wanderers, carried along unconsciously by the prevalent currents forever. Only reflection, the kind of directed reflection that questions the very basis of our habits and assumptions, could lead us out of wandering and towards understanding, towards deliberate action, towards emancipation.

The silver lining to the heart attack was that I was cast outside my usual currents and flung into solitude and uncertainty. The path of my cyclical wandering had been broken.

———

During my last few days in the ICU, my mind kept returning to that moment on the hike – to how serene it was on the mountain path, and how the funny, elusive question of value illuminated itself, for a fleeting moment, in the face of death.

Almost every night that I slept in the ICU, I had recurring dreams about hiking somewhere. On one of the first nights, I dreamt that my companions and I had reached the top of a mountain. We were peering down through the fog, marvelling at the landscape below. Everyone was exhausted, and eager to simply sit down and bask in the view. Nobody moved.

Until a companion amongst us spoke up. 'Come on, guys. To see the next peak, we must descend from this one.'

2

INHERITED VALUES

———————❖———————

LEAVING the hospital for the first time, I cherished the simplest of sensations: to walk on the pavement, to hear the deafening sounds of Mumbai traffic, to feel the light rain warmed by the afternoon sun like an ointment on my skin. Upon my return home, I was greeted by a crowd of family and friends, each bearing good wishes and a dessert of some kind, until soon my kitchen was filled with vats of Indian desserts such as payasam, ladoo and my childhood favourite, gulab jamun, soft, sugary balls of mawa and maida flecked with my mother's own touch: pieces of coconut and a pinch of cardamom.

There were tears in my eyes, a feeling of rejuvenation from this outpouring of love. Yet, as the days went by and my cousins, aunts, uncles, parents and friends trickled back to their own homes and lives, I also felt relieved. There was a sense of unfinished business from the ICU, some thread that I had grasped briefly but which slipped out of reach again, overshadowed by family lunches, phone conferences, planning, conversations, the unending stimulus of reality...

Now that I was alone, I tried to take up the thread again, starting with that slippery concept – value. A value is defined as something you regard as important, worthy, useful. A value is also a principle or standard by which you judge what is important in your life. Values are not created in tabula rasa; they are rarely original ideas etched on a blank slate. On the contrary, most values are *transmitted*, whether openly or subtly, slowly or quickly. And values can become so deeply embedded that they function as a seamless part of your thinking and doing, until it seems as if they must have just *been* there all along. Being able to critically analyse a value system, or a set of propositions, requires active training, not necessarily through formal education. The search for hidden assumptions and biases is an intuition that must be sharpened with practice.

As individuals, we do not exist alone in a vacuum, and our system of values does not either. Most of us would like to think that we stick to our self-chosen values, but it is impossible to account for the intersubjective and inter-temporal aspects of value. Simply put, we value things that others around us (and society, more generally) value, and we value (or refuse to value) that which has been passed down through time.

I wondered how much of what I valued and how I chose to value anything was inherited, and if so, from which influences and sources I may have inherited it. To explain why this story eventually takes us to a certain kind of valuing, I needed to travel into the past.

———

My grandfather's name was Bontiah Kailas. He was a merchant who grew up in a small village about 150 kilometres from Hyderabad. During the Depression years of the mid-1930s, opportunities in his village were steadily declining – harvests were poor, grain and milk prices were low, and many families were struggling to make ends meet.

This economic depression affected communities across India, prompting a mass migration of people in search of livelihood. Roads were clogged with rickshaws and caravans carrying villagers and their handmade belongings from their rural settlements to the cities, where they looked for new prospects. With a wife and two young sons to feed, my grandfather decided to move to Hyderabad, the closest city. My father, Sree Ramulu Kailas, was his second son.

My grandparents were from the Vaishya – or merchant and artisan – caste. In cities, the Vaishyas traditionally lived and conducted business in one concentrated area. In Hyderabad this area was called General Bazaar, a dynamic market near the centre of the city that survives to this day – an area humming with energy, and packed with stalls showcasing rows and rows of gold bangles, hair bands, souvenirs and cloth. In my grandfather's time, a few of our relatives were already living and trading in General Bazaar.

'Come, join us!' They wrote to my grandfather. 'You can work alongside your family and learn the ways of the city.'

But my grandfather had a different idea. Although India was still under British rule in the mid-1930s, Hyderabad operated as a semi-autonomous princely state. The British did not govern it directly, but shared power with the Nizam of Hyderabad, whose family had ruled the city for centuries. At the time my grandfather moved into the city, the Nizam was undertaking the ambitious project of building an internationally renowned university, the first of its kind in Hyderabad. It would be known as Osmania University.

In an unorthodox yet crucial move, my grandfather decided not to join his relatives and fellow Vaishyas in General Bazaar. Instead, he settled in Tarnaka, where the Nizam's university was being built.

With this singular act, he changed the course of my family's life.

Tarnaka was not an established locality like General Bazaar, but an up-and-coming area. Settling there, in an undeveloped neighbourhood, and without his Vaishya community around him, was deemed a highly risky endeavour by my grandfather's relatives. But land in Tarnaka was relatively cheap, and my grandfather believed there would be an influx of people moving into the area. So, he set up a small corner shop across the street from the university-under-construction, where he sold basic goods like rice and other groceries. Some of his earliest customers were construction workers from the university, who would stop by for their daily staples.

My grandfather built a home shortly after setting up his store. It was not really a home in the way most of us think of it, but a small room attached to the storefront, separated from the shop only by a light blue cloth. In that one room, my grandparents raised ten children – seven sons and three daughters. In that one room, a family of twelve ate, slept, lived and dreamed.

As my grandfather settled with his growing family in Tarnaka, India was going through one of its most definitive historical and political eras. The Second World War was ending and India was emerging from the final ripples of the Great Depression. A huge wave of urban migration was taking place. The freedom movement against British colonial rule was gaining traction across the country, the spark of change was ignited by the nationwide tour of villages and cities by Mahatma Gandhi, who carried with him the vision of Indian independence after the war. In 1947, that dream was fulfilled. India gained independence, ending nearly 200 years of British rule.

On the eve of Independence, Jawaharlal Nehru, the first prime minister of India and an outstanding leader of the freedom movement, gave his famed 'Tryst with Destiny' speech. 'At the stroke of the midnight hour, when the world sleeps,' he proclaimed to an electrified crowd, 'India will awake to life and freedom.'

With Independence, India suddenly became the largest political experiment in modern history: a newly decolonized state that had now become the most populous democracy in the world. Many scholars, politicians and leaders warned how India – with its enormous population, low income, poor literacy and history of social conflict between different religions and castes – would dissolve into dictatorship or sectarian conflict within a decade of Independence.

Given the violence and trauma of Partition, these warnings seemed even more justified. Partition was designed by the

British to 'protect' the Muslim minority in the country, but its hasty implementation only amplified religious strain as huge populations of Muslims across the Indian subcontinent streamed towards Pakistan on the western border, and a smaller number to what is now Bangladesh on the eastern border, without any aid or support. The British had left seemingly overnight, and the newly formed Indian government had yet to fill its vacuum: both had failed to protect the most vulnerable of their people.

My grandfather told us stories of the communal riots in the streets of Hyderabad, where crowds paraded through the city, supporting removal of the Nizam. The mutilated bodies of young men were strewn in the streets; Muslim stores were looted and their storefronts smashed to bits. He would recount to us stories of families fleeing from Hyderabad to Pakistan, and how he, as a devout Hindu, would spare some dal or rice for the crying mothers who passed the shop, most of them having little more than the clothes on their back, to sustain them through their migration. *These are our neighbours,* he would say. *Our neighbours are being killed by neighbours. We have let the British divide us. We have allowed hatred into our hearts.* Across the country, nearly 14 million were displaced by Partition, and many more perished in the violence. Independence had been won, it seemed, at a very high cost.

The months and years following Indian independence saw an amalgamation of hope and despair, formation and destruction, faith and hatred. It was a time of extreme transformation and uncertainty. Yet, against all expectations, India survived. To this day, despite its many flaws, the country remains a sovereign democracy.

At the time of Independence, the spirit of hope and experimentation that filled the country was so intense that it could not be completely quashed by the traumatic Partition that the British left behind in their wake. It was, as Nehru said, 'a moment which comes but rarely in history, when we step out from the old to the new, when an age ends, and when the soul of a nation, long suppressed, finds utterance.'

His voice, sonorous and prophetic, rang throughout India, and from the paan shops to the havelis, from the villages to the cities, we huddled around that voice, around that promise of a renewed destiny. It was an imperfect destiny, but it was finally ours.

My father grew up in this period of familial and national transformation. Working in my grandfather's shop during the day, he met professors and students from the newly established Osmania University. The people from the university became his window to the world. He overheard their discussions about the freedom movement, their debates on politics, their hushed and worried conversations about literature exams and engineering labs. He marvelled as they came in and tried to fit the dals they had bought into bags which were bursting with books. To my father, these professors and students were what he could aspire to be: knowledgeable, confident and purposeful.

My grandfather, however, was still extremely bound to tradition. He, as well as my grandmother, had had no formal education, and they actively discouraged my father and their other children from an education, believing it would diminish their loyalty to the family shop. This was the traditional Vaishya mindset. The children were trained in basic chores, and when they were old enough, were meant to work in the family business. Children milked cows, tended to the shop or found some job outside the house to make a living. An education was unnecessary and seen as a costly waste of time.

As the second son in a family of ten children, my father gradually took on a quasi-parental role with the rest of his siblings. Even though his brothers and sisters certainly did not appreciate his domineering attitude at times, they gave in to his commands. My father never considered his life as an individual, but as an existence that was bound, inextricably, to that of the larger unit of his family. But with time he grew resentful of his family's rejection of education or of any life beyond the family shop. He believed it robbed his siblings of a chance at a better life. This conviction grew in his heart, planting the seeds of his rebellion.

'Why can't we go to school, like other children in Tarnaka?' he would ask his mother while sweeping the shop floor after closing hour.

'*Beta*, why *would* you go to school? Did I raise and feed you for all these years so that you can run away and read books? Where is your gratitude? How will we live without your help around here?'

'We only have this tiny shop. Why do we need ten children to run one tiny shop?'

My grandmother, hearing this, would swat him for impertinence. 'Tiny shop!' She huffed, 'We would not be such a tiny shop if all of you actually contributed!'

My father simply could not accept those shop walls as the boundaries of his life. At fifteen, he left home, breaking the sacred bond of the Vaishya tradition. Instead of tending to the shop, he found a part-time job as a clerk at a government agency.

He worked during the day and enrolled for commerce classes in the evening. He openly fought against his parents and, much to their horror, hatched a plan with his younger brothers and sisters so they could enrol in school as well.

My grandmother did not stand by idly through my father's rebellion – she tried to thwart his efforts, either forbidding his siblings from seeing him, or spreading rumours about his reputation among the Vaishya community so that my father would not be able to receive any outside help.

Soon the time of year came for official registration at the local school. My father recollects sitting under a tree in the courtyard of the school with his brothers and sisters. Since they had no official records – poor families often lacked documentation such as birth certificates – he decided to make a fun ritual out of picking birthdays for himself and for each of his siblings.

It was a rare moment of magic, when the silent harshness that my father had built as an armour softened.

'I can pick *any* day?' my father's youngest sister asked him, tugging at his arm with a wide-eyed look.

'Yes, any day.'

'Can I pick an important day?'

'You can pick any day,' my father replied. She giggled and counted on her fingers before finally deciding on 26 January, India's Republic Day.

It must have been a funny sight, my father leading a gaggle of his siblings to the local school, each proudly holding a sheet of paper with their names and new birthdays. When the registration officer asked for their father's name, there was a sudden pause, each child falling silent. The registration officer did not notice their sudden stiffening, and asked again for their father's name. My father gave his own.

———

Whenever I asked my father how he was able to make this radical decision at that very young age, following it through with his obsession for education, even though it meant deviating from generations of tradition, he would point out three reasons.

'The first,' he said, 'was that your grandfather did not live in General Bazaar. It was not his intention, but moving to Tarnaka meant that we were not stuck in the traditional Vaishya ecosystem.' That move brought my father exposure to educated people attending university, opening the horizons of his imagination and dreams.

The second reason was the infectious air of experimentation and hope that permeated post-Independence India. Old barriers were being brought down and previous structures of power were in the process of being overturned and rewritten. All this called for bold voices unafraid of change.

'Boundaries were disrupted every day,' my father said. 'I would often learn this from the newspapers that the government officials left in the waste bin after work. Every day, such stories! India was an independent country. We were drawing the borders of Indian states and writing the Indian Constitution. The Indian people were on the world stage.'

Suddenly, even for a young boy from the outskirts of an Indian city, the 'world historical' came into one's own reality, leaving its mark and smell on people, on entire cities, until it travelled its way to the slums of Tarnaka.

The third reason, my father said, was simple: our family was poor. He explained that this meant we had to seek opportunities for social betterment at every turn. Poverty meant that we were not bound to tradition the way wealthier Vaishyas tended to be. Indeed, if the working and middle-class Vaishyas in General Bazaar found it difficult to look past their traditional way of life, wealthy Vaishyas had an even harder time breaking out of their customs and routines.

With this comment, my father was referring to the Vaishya custom of wealth accumulation, which was to take some money from the family business every year and invest it in some other type of asset – land, gold, or any comparable store of value. Over the generations, after twenty or thirty years of accumulation, some of those assets became very valuable. In fact, most of the financial worth of a wealthy Vaishya family came (more often than not) through passive income (in the form of rents on land, for instance) from these accumulated assets rather than from the profits of their operational businesses.

The wealth transfer system through which later generations inherited these family assets anchored them in a certain way of life. On the one hand, this was a good thing, because families became self-sufficient and prosperous, living a stable existence from generation to generation. On the other hand, this strongly deterred deviation from the status quo – family members, even if they wanted to pursue other paths, did not leave the business out of fear of losing their right to these assets. Throughout the generations, passive wealth pooled and concentrated in the hands of a few families, which intermarried with other such families in an open bid to combine 'complementary' assets. In a young and budding country like India, this created massive inequalities, which mark our society up to the present day. Vaishyas who owned large plots of land lived in luxury in secured mansions just kilometres away from the Vaishya shop owners and common merchants who slept in the slums of Hyderabad.

We were poor, my father said, but we were free. Often, wealth could become a sort of yoke that deterred you from the vibrancy of change, that stopped you from planting the seeds of risk that one day might flourish into a completely new life. Exposure to a university setting, the backdrop of political change in India, and the absence of inherited wealth, all contributed to my father's and his siblings' ability to break away from the past and forge a new life for themselves.

My father's decision turned out for the best, and the education that he and my uncles and aunts received eventually secured a completely different future for my family. In the end, all my father's younger siblings attended university. Seven of them emigrated to the United States, becoming entrepreneurs and professionals in their own right. Even though each set off on his or her own, each arriving in America with little more than $100 and a whole lot of uncertainty, all of them have achieved considerable success in their professional and personal lives.

In a single generation, the Kailas family went from owning a corner shop in Tarnaka to becoming a family of computer retailers, real estate developers, hospitality businessmen, doctors, engineers, lawyers and teachers.

The key, my father repeated, lies in harnessing the ability to step back from your frame of reference, much of which was not chosen but inherited in the random lottery of circumstance. Custom and tradition were important for certain reasons, and wealth too was desirable for certain reasons, but it was vital to understand how these things distorted your perspective, obstructing other possible ways of living and being. For most people, though, the birth lottery creates a rigid narrative in the mind that is used to assign cause and effect, to explain life and to move through existence, emphasizing only those things that corroborate their own world view and ignoring much else. This type of confirmation bias was dangerous, yet invisible.

My father was, without question, the man who commanded the most respect in my life, the man whose influence has left an indelible and eternal mark on me. He was not a particularly warm man, but he was deliberate and kind – everything that he did was for a well-calculated reason. My mother, on the other hand, was his perfect foil, a woman known for her affectionate and cheerful personality. She was the kind of person who would leave flowers by my bed when she sensed I was stressed. Together, my father and my mother were like two halves of one consciousness, two intertwined orbits.

When I was ten, my father took me and my sister Uma for a drive through Tarnaka. He believed, even in that era, that the son and daughter should be given the same experiences. There was no inequality when it came to us, no separate realities. My sister thus became my ultimate ally and confidante – her organized and studious tolerance of me remains one of the greatest and most inexplicable gifts of my family.

Even though both my sister and I had been living in Tarnaka for nearly a decade, neither of us knew that just three minutes' drive from our house lay the slum where he grew up. We walked through the cluster of tin houses and debris without saying a word.

Then my father stopped in front of a small hut, and broke the silence. 'Beta,' he said, looking at both of us, 'This was where our house used to be, where I lived with all your uncles and aunties.'

'*All* of you?' It did not seem like the room could comfortably house more than four adults.

'Yes, all of us. This is where we came from.'

I did not know what to say. But my father continued, 'And I am going to tell you something now that I told each of your uncles and aunties too.'

'What is it, Daddy?'

'Listen closely, beta. You must understand that the only thing that I can give either of you is an education. Whether that is at school, or through working with me, a few grains of knowledge about this life are the only thing I can try to give you.'

He paused, then added, 'You are my son. But you must live your own life. I will help you with an education, but that is all. I cannot give you a job, a business, a source of wealth. I also cannot give you a belief system, a path. All this you must find for yourself.'

My father stuck to his word. And I think he shared this with me when I was so young because he wanted this to be ingrained knowledge. When I left for Mumbai, he did not pressure me to stay and work with him in his businesses. Likewise, he never invested in any of my companies, which was highly peculiar for an Indian 'business' family. Besides a small loan that I repaid within a few months while finding my footing in Mumbai, he did not give me any money. He would have been happy to support me if I had asked, but the tacit understanding between us was that we must honour independence above everything else. His love was unwavering and unquestioning, and this was his greatest gift to me: the freedom to find and define my own path.

———

Looking out on Marine Drive from my bedroom window in Mumbai, I was overcome by the memory of that day at the slum; it was as sharp as if it were yesterday. My father had long ago taught me that you always needed to cross-examine your own life, put it up to a mirror and ask: What am I seeing? What am I not seeing? What can I change? There was certainly an emptiness to my life, a lack of purpose, a dissatisfaction with entrepreneurship as I practised it. The need for cross-examination was clear.

Perhaps the most important value I inherited from my father was that his life was not his own, but a continual act of dedication to his family. His family was his duty, his source of value, his driving force and his purpose in life. And the family was only one unit beyond the individual self; this strand of thinking can be expanded to society as a whole.

'Vasudhaiva kutumbakam' is a Sanskrit phrase found in the Upanishads that outline core Hindu teachings. Vasudhaiva kutumbakam: the world is one family. I would come back to this phrase, later, in my search for a different kind of value.

Funny, now that my own life had pushed me into a state where I could no longer ignore core questions of purpose and being, these memories resurfaced like an omen. If my father could start anew in circumstances that were so difficult, if he was able to take such risks with everything to lose, then I too should find the inner strength to question the customs and traditions I had built into my own life.

Within a few months I had closed or sold all three of my businesses and left Mumbai.

3

THE ART OF TANGENTIAL SOLUTIONS

❖

TO understand how difficult it was for me to leave Mumbai, you have to understand that my businesses were my life. Entrepreneurship was not something that I pursued out of love for wealth or social standing. To me it was an act of creation in which I found the most complete state of dedication and joy.

'An artist is someone who finds a space, enters it, and works.' For most of my early career, my entrepreneurial philosophy mirrored the artist's creative mindset. The world was a canvas of hidden opportunity, and the entrepreneur's role was to identify opportunities and build something with a mixture of analytical skill and creative self-expression.

Like an artist, I had to find a space, enter it, and work. And just the way exceptional artists have a distinctive style and talented writers possess a singular authorial voice, so too does the creative entrepreneur have the capacity to develop his or her own special mark of creation. I prided myself on a particular style of doing business, which I called the tangential approach.

A tangent is a straight line or plane that touches a curve at one point. The tangential approach, in my mind, sought out solutions that did not answer a problem head-on or by brute force, but by engaging with the problem peripherally, *just grazing* the problem, the same way a tangent lightly touched, yet did not intersect, a circle's edge.

Tangential solutions were unexpected and clever; they did not require size or strength, but elegance and tact. To me, they were the mark of the underdog.

———

Although my early ventures were across various industries and utilized very different business models, their essential kernel was the same. I thought of myself as an individual entrepreneur in search of tangential solutions.

When I moved to Mumbai in 1996 to first try my hand at entrepreneurship, the telecommunications industry in India was in the process of revolution. In 1994, India unveiled what is now known as the New Telecom Policy (NTP), which replaced the Indian Telegraph Act of 1885. The NTP outlined a process for issuing licences and slowly deregulating the telecommunications sector; it was the first significant policy that shifted the balance of power in telecommunications from the government to the private sector.

I saw this as an incredible opportunity, perhaps the most significant opportunity in India at the time. With landline and mobile phone penetration at such low levels, there were hundreds of millions of untapped consumers whose lives could be significantly improved by landlines, mobile phones and other telecommunication services. However, all the industry players who were attracted to the telecommunications sector were giant multinational companies (AT&T, General Motors, the Tatas) with enormous amounts of capital at their disposal.[1] These companies were bidding for licences to operate Indian phone lines, to the tune of billions of dollars. I was just a kid who had freshly arrived from Hyderabad, living in a gritty hotel at the edge of the city, with no experience in the industry and no capital of my own.

As becoming an official licensee was prohibitively capital-intensive, I rationalized that the best way to enter this market was to provide some service within the telecommunications industry. My first idea, to create a calling-cards business for making calls overseas, failed after a year. The grand plans that I had for my entrepreneurial life in Mumbai fizzled out, and so did my fantasy about my predestined fame and fortune. I was brought down to reality. In the afternoons, I ate stale rotis alone in the Mumbai hotel, avoiding the corridors where less-than-honourable characters and their visitors lurked.

But entrepreneurship should be experienced as a continuum, as a process with no determinate end, and one important skill is to treat it as such. Businesses fail much more often than they succeed, yet the entrepreneur should view the trajectory of his or her own ventures as a constantly challenged evolution. The process takes precedence over the product, the means over the ends. The real failure is to disrupt or lose faith in the continuum and not to be able summon the strength to get up again after defeat.

I plunged myself back into research, looking for another window of opportunity in the telecom industry. I soon found that the telecom giant, Hughes Communications, then a division of General Motors, was bidding to become a major licensee in India. To negotiate their deal with the Department of Telecommunications, Hughes had sent a team of thirty top managers from their Washington D.C. headquarters to Mumbai. They were all staying at the Oberoi, one of the most luxurious hotels in Mumbai.

My strategy was simple. I would go to the Oberoi right before the breakfast buffet opened, set up my gigantic 1990s-brick-laptop on a desk in the lobby and begin to work 'casually' upon their seeing me. When the Hughes entourage passed by on their way to breakfast, I would look up, make eye contact, and smile.

'Good morning!' I waved enthusiastically, as the contingent walked past the first day.

'Good morning,' a few of them would grumble, while the others silently hurried towards their morning coffee.

As the days passed I added another layer to my stealth operation and started going to the Oberoi for a post-work drink too. At first I would sit with a drink by myself, taking care to nod and smile if any Hughes personnel passed by.

'Say, what are you doing here all the time?' a junior vice president in sales asked me one evening, breaking the ice. I had finally been recognized as a friendly and familiar face – in this instance, both 'friendly' *and* 'familiar' are key.

'I'm in-between things right now,' I responded. 'But I work as an entrepreneur. What do you do? There seems to be quite a crowd here.' I gestured to the crowd of Hughes personnel hovering around the bar.

'We all work at the same company.' He smiled. 'Hughes. Have you heard of it?'

'Hughes … ' I pretended to run the name through my memory. 'Satellites?'

'In the States, yes. I was living in DC before I got pulled into this whole outfit, but now it looks like we'll hunkering down here for a while. Hughes is trying to get involved in the telecommunications industry in India, given the entire regulatory overhaul.'

'Tell me more,' I replied quickly. 'I'd love to learn about the industry.'

In this way, over the course of two months, I developed a credible relationship with some of the senior managers at the company. Now all I had to do was to come up with a business idea to put that relationship to use.

———

I had got into the habit of taking a bus or train to visit the villages outside Mumbai on the weekends. Like hiking, it was a way to clear my mind of the city's commotion. The villages of India are completely different from the cities. Rural life was – and still remains – the pulse of the country.

One weekend, it struck me that villagers in India were people and consumers that companies like Hughes ignored since they were too poor to afford landlines or mobile phones. Hughes targeted top-notch, paying customers, traditionally corporate and urban, who offered the highest revenue per phone line. I began to think … is there a way to provide a good service to these disadvantaged communities? Could I build a competitive company that serviced this demographic?

In 1994 there were no mobile phones in India, and less than 5 per cent landline penetration.[2] Still, the need to communicate with others was not restricted to corporations or wealthy urban populations. People without enough money to have their own landline phones mostly communicated using payphones. Payphones had not only enabled urban-rural migration and communication, but had also allowed farmers in distant areas to more efficiently update with their suppliers, customers and other farmers within a large geographical area.

With time, payphones became a popular small business, not only in only rural India but also in urban neighbourhoods. Across Indian cities, you could find payphone operators sitting in their miniature stalls on the street, guarding a phone attached to a meter. When the call ended, the payphone would print a small bill that was then collected by the operator. Because payphones dealt with multiple consumers per line, margins in this business were much higher than in the traditional landlines business. Payphones accounted for less than 1 per cent of the total number of phone lines in India at the time, but brought nearly 15 per cent of the revenues.

To me, the opportunity in India lay in its massive market. We were a poor country, but we were growing and modernizing at an incredible rate. Without legacy infrastructure, we were able to leapfrog technologies – skipping to the newest and best versions without having to bear any replacement costs. Yet, while most businesses, especially non-Indian businesses, focused on the wealthiest portion of the population – the educated, urban middle class – I always felt there would be enormous value (in terms of profit and human value) in providing services to the most disadvantaged sectors of society. With a bit of creativity, one could build a profitable, competitive business that serviced those with the least means.

Zip Telecom was the name of the payphone company I incorporated in 1996. We eventually became the world's largest independent payphone company, with almost 25,000 installations across India. However, at the time of its inception, we were teetering on shaky ground. As I mentioned earlier, at that point I had no capital, no experience in raising capital and no experience in telecommunications. The main question I faced was, how would we compete against giant telecommunications companies as sophisticated as Hughes? How would we attract talent to a payphone operation if most people with a telecommunications background flocked for employment to these large and credible companies?

This was my first experiment with tangential solutions. I reasoned that while I could attack the problem head-on, that is, simply try to build and grow a payphone company that worked like Hughes and competed with Hughes, the results would be suboptimal. The way to remain competitive would be to start a company in the telecommunication space, but one that *did not operate* like a telecommunications company. I spent three months pitching the idea to distributors of fast-moving consumer goods (FMCG) in Mumbai, and raised enough capital to begin building the company.

With Zip Telecom, I focused on two tangential sources of revenue. The first was advertising. While it seems obvious today, in 1996 we were an early proponent of the business model that incorporated unrelated, generalist advertising as a major revenue source from a technology product. To advertise effectively, we decided to design our own state-of-the-art payphone. I envisioned a payphone with a beautiful digital display for advertising, multiple functionalities, and perhaps even Web browsing. But our first design cost $3,000 per phone, whereas our competitors used basic payphones that only cost $250 per unit.

The way to solve this problem, I decided, was not to think of our product as a payphone. We had been dealing with payphone designers, component sellers and vendors. The 'dumb boxes' we could find on every street corner in New York and London were payphones. What we were building was, in fact, not a payphone, but a computer in a phone package. Computers had far more functionality, something I was keen not to sacrifice in our product, yet computer components were much cheaper than phone components as a result of recent innovations in the computer chip industry. I told our head of design to proceed with that thinking, and to use computer parts rather than the standard phone components to build our prototype.

In three months we came out with a prototype of the most technologically advanced payphone in the world, which was price-competitive with the $250 metered and manned pay phones on the streets of Mumbai. The phone, much to my glee, had the digital screen I had originally envisioned, which we used as a rotational advertising platform. Utilizing advertising as a secondary source of revenue on equipment that performed a different function was my tangential solution to the problem of cracking the revenue question in the telecommunications industry.

The second tangential solution that I utilized was franchising. Since most of these payphones were operated by small stalls and mom-and-pop stores, franchising was a logical model. But franchising also had its drawbacks; it meant we needed to build a company well equipped to deal with thousands of individual owners. Questions abounded: how would we effectively collect money from every owner? How could we interface with them at a low cost? Pacing around in Mumbai, I realized that the most common parallel to our business was the distribution industry that was already in existence in India. The companies that distributed, say, FMCG products like Coke, Pepsi, or Cadbury chocolates, already had established networks for working with millions of small and large retailers, from street stalls to department stores.

The most successful distribution story in India at the time was Pepsi. Indeed, India was the only sizeable country where Pepsi was the market leader over Coke. This was primarily due to a small local management team of Pepsi's, a squadron of distribution veterans and super-smart marketers. With a budget that was less than half of Coke's, the Pepsi team clocked more sales than their chief competitor throughout the 1990s.[3]

That caught my attention. So, I went to their executive director of franchising, Shishir Lall, and asked him to work for Zip Telecom. Neither of us knew that he would eventually lead Zip Telecom to its global success. After many weeks of tireless chasing, I finally managed to get Shishir to agree to meet me in Goa, where he was attending a wedding. I could see that he was both perturbed and amused by this slightly dishevelled-looking twenty-nine-year-old who was trying to convince him to leave a top executive job at the height of his professional career to join a startup operation with no capital of its own.

But this is the most exciting industry of the decade, I pitched to him. And we are building a company within the most exciting industry in India that needs *exactly* the set of skills you built at Pepsi. Trying to build our payphone company from scratch would be a challenge, there was no doubt about that, but it was a challenge with meaningful personal and professional payoffs.

At one point, Shishir, again with the half-amused expression on his face, took a sip of his mango lassi, thought for a long moment, then finally asked, 'How are you going to afford to pay my salary?'

I laughed aloud, dispelling any remaining tension between us. 'That's exactly what I want to hire you to figure out!' Two months later, he formally joined our team. The rest, as they say, is history. Over the course of seven years, we became India's first venture-backed company, raising over $25 million in the early 2000s, employed over 600 people, and became one of the most innovative payphone companies in the world.

———

While running and growing Zip Telecom, I was also becoming increasingly interested in the real estate sector in India. In the early 2000s, India was becoming the real back office to the world. The booming IT sector drew in multinational companies eager to set up offices in cities like Mumbai. The question on my mind was of the same nature as the one I had when starting Zip: given the enormous capital required to participate in the real estate sector, how could I pursue an opportunity in that space without adhering to the traditional business model? How could I apply a tangential solution within the real estate sector?

The first part of the Altius story is that I noticed two things that would work to my advantage if I entered this industry. On the one hand, companies like Dell and Microsoft did not want to own their offices in India outright, for accounting reasons; they strongly preferred to rent property. On the other hand, because of the banking laws in India at the time, banks were not allowed to own real estate. They could take over real estate if there was a default on a loan, and only had a narrow allowance for non-default real estate which, after a certain period, they were obligated to sell. Other structures that owned real estate in Europe and America, such as real estate investment trusts, were not yet legally acceptable in India.

I had discussed this conundrum with one of my friends over our many dinners together. Across Mumbai and Bangalore, we identified a few commercial buildings where large companies had signed ten- to fifteen-year leases to rent office space. The yield or profit from these rentals was between 15 per cent and 16 per cent, which was incredibly high, whereas the long-term interest rate (the cost of a long-term loan) in India was between 8 per cent and 9 per cent. Here lay a significant arbitrage opportunity: we could buy the real estate with a loan, pay 8 per cent or 9 per cent interest on the loan every year, and pocket the remaining revenues made from rental yields.

The only issue was my deep aversion to debt.

'I'm not sure about this,' I admitted, as we sketched out a plan for the company. 'You know, I watched my father really suffer because of the debt he took. Maybe that's why I'm so uncomfortable with it.' And indeed, significant debt did not figure in any of my businesses. As I contemplated this, my friend grew impatient.

'What I certainly do *not* want to do is miss out on this opportunity,' he said, shaking his head.

'There must be another way to do this without having to take on so much debt. That type of exposure is dangerous. We should find a way to own these buildings without owning them. Make profit without having debt.'

'Are you going off about your tangential solutions again?' My friend had heard my ramblings many times before.

'We will find another way.'

So, instead of buying the real estate outright, my friend and I created an options contract. In finance, an *option* is a contract which gives a buyer (the owner of the option) the right to buy or sell an asset at a specific price over a specific time period. So, we wrote a clever and legally complex contract by which banks would, effectively, be able to purchase the commercial buildings we identified. But since banks were only able to hold non-default real estate for a specified period, they signed an options contract that allowed my friend and me to buy back their portfolio of buildings in three years at the same price at which the banks had originally bought them. Our company, named Altius, consisted solely of Rs 10,000, or about $200 of incorporation costs (the cost of legally setting up the business) and one piece of paper – the options contract.[4]

I took pride in Altius because it was an efficient and elegant tangential solution to an opportunity we had identified. It seemed that all parties won: the owners of the buildings were happy since they got the money. The banks were happy since they indirectly yet legally owned the buildings and were earning fantastic rental yields. Three years later, much to the banks' surprise and much to our delight, the value of those buildings multiplied in value too, against all expectations. Mumbai's real estate market had reached new highs with each passing year.

So, three years later, just before the expiration of the contract, my friend and I sold Altius to a fund that was trying to diversify into real estate holdings.

Our profit was the property appreciation value, the difference between the options value and the market value of the properties. With one piece of paper, some structuring, a little bit of imagination and a couple meetings, my partner and I had made a serious profit, enough for many lifetimes.

Altius itself had no office, no employees and no product. It was simply a tangential solution.

———

The last tangential solution that I will discuss relates to my living arrangements in Mumbai. I always love this example, because I think it drives home the point that entrepreneurship is a continuum and not a discrete activity. An entrepreneurial mindset does not only apply in building businesses, but also in approaching all kinds of dilemmas that arise in life.

When I first arrived in Mumbai, the biggest hurdle was to find suitable housing. Apartments were extremely expensive to rent, with unfavourable terms that required one year's payment upfront and all kinds of guarantees. I visited a few places that were within my budget, but the buildings were old and located far from the centre of the city.

Then came the time when I was visiting the Oberoi frequently to stage my 'run-ins' with the Hughes team. One thing I noticed in the Oberoi was that the stack of newspapers in the hotel's lobby did not diminish, whatever the time of day. When I was younger, and was accompanying my father to the hotel for his Mumbai meetings, I remember asking a bellhop how many newspapers they had. Apparently the large, overflowing stack in the lobby would disappear in a few hours' time, vacuumed away by requests from hotel guests and visitors.

I deduced that the dot-com bust of the early 2000s must have hit the hotel hard. There were fewer customers, and corporate groups like the Hughes team would stay for a few months before finding permanent accommodation. So, one day I called the general manager, a grey-haired, serious man, over to my seat in the lobby. He already knew my face from my constant presence at the hotel. Little did he know that he was to become part of my tangential solution to the problem of living in Mumbai.

My proposal to him was simple. I was searching for an apartment in Mumbai, but could not find anything satisfactory. From my study of the Oberoi's balance sheet, I could tell that their profits had been declining sharply for the past eighteen months. The hotel was suffering its lowest occupancy rates in a decade. Long-term borrowing costs were rising, which strained finances even further. I told the manager that under these circumstances, I had an offer he could not refuse. I was willing to be their *long-term* customer: I would be happy to sign a contract to stay in the hotel for six continuous years, if they agreed to give me a massive discount.

The general manager, unsurprisingly, found this proposal preposterous. I was asking to live in the most luxurious hotel in Mumbai, right on Marine Drive, for a lesser amount than I would pay to rent a two-bedroom apartment on the outskirts of the city. And I was not going to settle for living in a room, but requested four hotel suites to be combined into an eight-room residential apartment, the first of its kind in the Oberoi.

When the general manager asked to see my personal finances, I relented, but warned him that he was not going to be impressed.

It took nearly seven months of negotiations before I wore down the general manager's initial reluctance. I supplied revenue projections showing how long-term premium guests could contribute more value when there were fewer holiday or business customers at the hotel. I vowed to hold all my business meetings in the Oberoi and promote the hotel within my network. I even offered granting the hotel access to my bespoke apartment for celebrity guests – I would simply stay with a friend on those days (fun fact, the only time they took advantage of this clause was when Michael Jackson stayed at the hotel for two evenings, many years later). But most of all, I think the general manager and the staff of the hotel simply liked me as a person. They were amused by my enthusiasm, realized that the numbers did not make the deal *impossible*, and finally gave in.

In the end, we signed a contract for a six-year lease, with a price point that was within 10 per cent of my original proposal. Giddy with victory about my first home – a not-too-shabby one, I may add – I included all sorts of miscellaneous clauses in the rental agreement, starting with a request for twelve newspapers delivered to my doorstep every morning. I also wanted roses, colour-coordinated with each room and replaced every day. Lastly, and perhaps most importantly, I was to be given a lifetime's supply of rabri, a dessert made from sweet condensed milk, made available twenty-four hours a day on demand.

The Oberoi became my first real home and the site of many memories for my family. I still remember that when my son Daman was born, the hospital asked for his permanent address. Room 2601, Oberoi Towers, Mumbai, I wrote. The hospital nurse was incredulous. 'Your *permanent* address, sir. What you have written is the Oberoi.'

'That is my permanent address,' I laughed. They did not believe me until the general manager sent a personal letter confirming that it was indeed my address.

Daman quickly became the favourite of the hotel staff. Often, when I came home from work he would still be gone from the apartment, taken on some adventure with the Oberoi staff, only to return before dinner time with stories and gifts. When I was researching for this book, I revisited the Oberoi again, and everyone still asked about 'the little prince'.

————

As an entrepreneur, I saw myself as someone attempting to construct elegance in the midst of chaos. Tangential solutions were the only form of art I knew – I was seeking out solutions and patterns that others had not yet discerned, and creating opportunities out of them.

Yet, something was amiss. While I had always known, and accepted, that entrepreneurship itself was a highly demanding activity for any individual, somehow creating tangential solutions no longer moved me after my time in the ICU. I felt a certain detachment settle in, a chilling at the very core of my being. Solving puzzles for my own enjoyment, and as an outlet for my creative energy, suddenly paled. Why did the cherished tangential solutions of my past suddenly seem meaningless and diminished? Why did they leave me to more emptiness than ever before?

The only way to discover why, I decided, was to leave everything behind.

4

EXIT STRATEGY

———————❖———————

MY decision to leave Mumbai was met with enormous resistance. It was not a gentle murmur or suggestion of dissent, but a cry from most people I knew that my choice verged on the insane.

The first to express discontent at my choice was, ironically, my father. 'How will you ever re-enter business?' he whispered into the phone. 'What has gotten into you? It is difficult enough to build something like you did in the last few years. How will you get so lucky again?' His message was clear: don't squander away your blessings.

At the base of his disapproval was bafflement at my reason for leaving everything behind. 'What do you mean you want to *reflect* on the *value* of what you are doing? Life is about doing, beta. Nothing will be achieved if you sit and think for too long.'

He reminded me of a quotation attributed to the American writer Philip K. Dick: 'The problem with introspection, alas, is that it has no end.'

I did not know what to say to that.

The only person who supported the decision was my wife, Charita, who rejoiced that I would finally be stepping away from the business that had overshadowed our family life.

Despite the chorus of opinions around me, this was one of those decisions whose balance simply could not be tipped easily. I had decided to step away from everything, and I would still do so despite all the objections in the world.

———

Exiting a business with minimal loss, like building a business, required creative thinking, and tact too. It called for a certain degree of sensitivity, in order that one does not end up burning any bridges during the transition. I made the decision to walk away from active entrepreneurship, but I was still responsible for the employees, investors and partners involved in my ventures.

Luckily, during that year the telecommunications industry was on a high and the investor outlook positive. Within two months I had sold Zip Telecom to Tata Teleservices, one of the largest private telecommunications companies in India. Much to my relief, the employees and operations of Zip Telecom were almost entirely retained, and ownership of the company was shifted to the Tata conglomerate with minimal turmoil. The deal took nearly eight months to execute, but in the end, I felt I had fulfilled my responsibility to my employees.

I still remember my last meetings with Ro during the last weeks before selling Zip.

'I think I am going to return the unused portion of our last round of funding,' I told him, as I cleaned out my desk, which was nearly empty except for a few papers and stationery. A clear desk for a clear mind. I hated desks cluttered with old awards or plaques from the past.

'Why would you do that, Ravi?'

'Since I am the one who is walking away, Ro. For personal reasons that have nothing to do with any of the other stakeholders in this business.' Maintaining goodwill, in the long run, was far more important than walking away with the money.

'But Ravi,' his eyes widened, 'I'm speaking now as a friend, not an investor. You are the majority stakeholder in this company, which is not a small feat. This isn't a few extra bucks we are talking about, this is serious money.' He looked at me with an amused expression. 'Are you sure you want to give that away? Back to the investors?' He already knew my answer.

I wrapped up my other two businesses too in due time. I sold Xius, a company that delivered the world's first inter-operator, prepaid roaming service, to another telecom software corporation. And finally, I was in talks to sell my real estate options company, Altius, to a real estate investment group looking for an entry point to the Indian market. Altius was a company that consisted solely of me, plus a few legal documents. I completed the last few meetings to close some pending items. Within a few weeks, Altius as I knew it ceased to exist.

During this entire process, I was cheerily going to the office and continuing my usual routine. Most of the people around me found my equanimity unnatural, but I thought it was quite the opposite. Disengagement has always been a required and fundamental part of the business mindset. As an entrepreneur, you must constantly face the possibility that what you began might end. I had shuttered more failed businesses than had I built successful ones, and I had learned over the years how to live with that risk.

Still, it was a strange feeling to confront the impermanence of things that seemed so deeply rooted in my existence. In two months, the businesses that defined the past decade of my life became relics of my past, either continuing as self-sustaining organisms or dissolving altogether. To say that I felt no anxiety or fear – that foreboding sense of *what if I regret this in the future?* – would be false. Yet there was a certain harmony deep within; I felt a deep peace, tinged with the adrenaline of anticipation. I had, to the best of my ability, given myself a blank slate, a new canvas, a set of questions on which to reflect …

———

For the next few years I was involved with little to no commercial activity. Instead, my life quietly meandered its way into an exploration of the unfulfilled goals I had accumulated through the years. I read, hiked, and concentrated on spending time with my son Daman and newly-born daughter, Aditi. I travelled to the US to visit my uncles in Milwaukee and New Orleans. After two years of this, my wife Charita and I quietly separated; even the 'reset' of my life had not been able to save our marriage.

I eventually returned to live in Hyderabad, and my old friends approached me with caution and unspoken worry, as if there lurked some mystery behind my reappearance. Much to their surprise, I moved into my father's home and settled into a modest and quiet routine. All in all, the pace and mood of my life were cerebral, tranquil.

Even as a child I preferred to live 'in my own head', as my sister would often teasingly tell me. I was strange; I was sociable to an extent, but at core I always tended towards brooding in solitude. When my friends were drinking beer and meeting girls after school, I would slink away and take a book with me to Golconda, the ruins of a twelfth-century fort in the old neighbourhood of Hyderabad. It was not a popular destination back then, so I was largely left to myself, spending countless hours wandering through the patches of grass growing between the broken stones of the fort. I would pass entire afternoons in the half-collapsed halls of the fort, which were alive with wildflowers, squirrels and graffiti. I loved to imagine the fort in its original splendour; I also loved its natural decay.

Fast-forward thirty years, and I was back in Golconda, again with a book in one hand. The only difference was that now I had a beer in the other. I noticed that more and more middle-class families were picnicking or just strolling about at the fort on the weekends, turning it into a playground of giddy, running children and or a park of aunties and uncles reclining on blankets on the grass. On the weekdays, I was left alone again to pace the ruin's hallowed grandeur by myself, much like I did throughout my childhood.

It seemed like everything had come a full circle. The fort. The solitude. The thinking.

———

Nisha, my best companion from my hiking retreats, called me one day to ask if I was ever going to return to Mumbai.

'Not in the foreseeable future,' I replied. 'There doesn't seem to be any reason for me to go back. I live a quiet life, and I'm close to the children.'

'So, for the rest of your life you are going to be a wanderer whose primary activities are visiting his children and reading novels in old forts?'

'It's not an old fort, it's an *ancient* fort. Plus, I'm reading non-fiction too.'

'Ravi, you're avoiding my question.' She was right, but I did not want to reveal to her how much this line of questioning unsettled me. It had been five years, and I felt no closer to answering the questions invoked in the ICU. This was still a waiting period, a limbo. I was paralysed, unable to plunge back into any kind of activity with the knowledge that I could not address the emptiness that had unshackled me from my old life.

I was an extremely private person, rarely sharing details of my life even amongst friends, often to my own detriment. But when I heard Nisha's voice – and Nisha was a dear friend whom I had not seen since I left Mumbai – I thought that perhaps I had kept too much hidden for far too long.

The floodgates broke, and I told her everything: how Charita and I had got divorced. How I made a trip to see the kids every weekend in Chennai. How I had read countless books – on philosophy, history, natural sciences – and contemplated on life for the past half-decade without getting any closer to understanding how I could define what was valuable and build a life around those tenets. I even told Nisha about a woman I had met recently, whom I was starting to develop feelings for, despite believing that love was nearly impossible at this stage in my life.

There was a great silence on the line after my outburst. Then I heard Nisha's light, lilting voice ask, 'Have you tried meditating again?'

I think she could hear the shake of my head through the phone. 'Well, Ravi,' she said, 'Trust me on this. This is probably the only advice I can give you. Try to meditate again. Just submit to the experience. I think it will really help you.' As a clincher to her proposal that I register for a course in Vipassana meditation, she added: 'You have so much time now that you can't even use that as an excuse!'

We laughed, and I told her that I would think about it, which in my mind meant that I would perhaps register in six months' time or a year. Except that the next day, Nisha sent me an email confirming my enrolment in the next ten-day Vipassana meditation course near Hyderabad. The start date was seven weeks later.

———

Until that phone call from Nisha, my first and only exposure to meditation had been when I was living in Mumbai. At the time, I had just started training for my first marathon. Every day I would wake up at five in the morning for a ten-kilometre run on Marine Drive.

With time, my running coach increased my training runs from ten kilometres to twenty, then to thirty, and finally to the full marathon distance of 42.195 kilometres. Everything was going well, except for the last ten kilometres, the final hour or so of the marathon. Every time I attempted the full trial marathon, my body would refuse to continue past the thirty-kilometre mark. Even though I knew my muscles possessed the strength to keep going, it felt as if my body was halting against my will, balking until I stopped and fell in an exhausted heap. This runner's block seemed insurmountable, recurrent; I felt like a Sisyphus carrying his boulder up the mountain side.

My coach stressed that this must be a psychosomatic response. Your body has the capacity to finish the run, but your mind is shutting down, he would say. And a psychosomatic issue could not be solved by any physical remedy. I would need to find a way to regain control over my mind. He recommended meditation.

So, in November 2003 I arrived at Igatpuri, the global headquarters of the Vipassana foundation. In the middle of the sixty-five-acre campus stood a giant pagoda, a golden dome surrounded by pink lotus-shaped pods where individual meditators sat to practise. Scattered around the pagoda were paths and wooden structures that made up the simple student accommodations. When I arrived, I was ushered into a room with the other students in my course, where two assistant teachers explained what we should expect over the next ten days.

Just submit to the experience, was what Nisha said then as well, when she learned that it would be my first meditation retreat. I gave her my assurance, but in reality, I was attending for a purely transactional purpose. I wanted to accomplish one thing, and one thing only: to complete my marathon. All other considerations – 'enlightenment' or personal transformation – were far from my mind.

This attitude meant that besides trying to meditate at the prescribed times, I did not adhere to many of the retreat's other rules. I ate separately from the other students, eating my dinner when they abstained from food after sunset. My justification to the assistant teachers was that my hypoglycemia required frequent eating to ensure that my blood sugar did not drop below a certain level, but in truth I did not want to disturb my marathon-training diet.

During the midday walks, when we were urged to retain the calmness of our mind with the help of light physical activity, I would slip behind the dormitories and into the open fields lining the compound, where I completed my usual conditioning exercises and half an hour of intense running. Sometimes I even fit in an early morning training session before the gong signalled the beginning of the day's meditation schedule. Exhausted mentally and physically by the end of the day, I would doze off during the videos ('discourses', they were called) we were supposed to watch in the evening.

In the end, I left my first Vipassana experience with some degree of inner serenity – the technique did help to quiet my mind. As predicted by my coach, after the retreat I no longer had trouble finishing the last leg of the full marathon training run.

A week later I completed my first full trial marathon without a pause. I could hardly believe it – the resistance I had felt in all my previous attempts had just faded away. The antidote had worked, and I was victorious. With my feet on the finish line of the marathon, the memory of the retreat faded away.

———

I was not alone in taking a transactional approach to meditation, using the technique just to fulfil a specific personal need. In fact, the popularization of meditation and 'mindfulness' techniques has promoted a transactional approach to such practices across the world. From yoga to transcendental meditation, ancient practices, boasted about for their effects on inner development and self-help, have been refashioned as commodity services, especially in places such as the United States and Europe.

I recall my surprise when I walked into the Citibank headquarters in midtown Manhattan one day and stumbled on the vice president, whom I was supposed to meet, sitting cross-legged on the floor in his office. A chant was playing from the speakers on his desk, and a few members of his team sat in a semicircle around him. They all seemed to be meditating. When the vice president finally opened his eyes, and saw me gawking by the door, he smiled.

'Weekly productivity booster,' he said. The team dispersed and went back to their desks. I, of course, was still trying to pick my jaw up from the floor.

In short, the popularization of such practices in the mass market promotes a clear-cut, transactional approach, where meditation is undertaken for a specific, isolated end goal, *without* sensitivity to, or understanding of, the practice's moral and spiritual dimensions. It appears that a certain demographic of overworked, overstressed urban professionals has flocked to meditation, seeing it as a sort of mental haven. C-suite executives in high-powered occupations like finance and consulting, in particular, have created an entire culture around meditation, jetting on the weekends to luxurious 'ashram getaways' in spiritual centres in India. The 'gurus' who teach these 'transcendental' meditation courses espouse freedom from worldly desire on the one hand and lure their customers into financing various business and real estate deals on the other.

Many other organizations and individuals are also employing such practices for their own ends. In the biomedical context, meditation is now applied therapeutically as a means of reducing depression, stress, anxiety or drug addiction. Lululemon sells yoga apparel and accessories, its brands named after or incorporating Sanskrit terms, to women all over the world at a hefty price. Some of its stores even have 'meditation centres' where you can sit in a stress-proof lounge and meditate using an iPhone app.

There are so many such examples that critics of this transactional approach to spiritual practices have termed the commodification of meditation into a 'banal, therapeutic, self-help technique' as 'McMindfulness,' a play on what is perhaps the most recognizable symbol of American capitalism.

I did not know all this then, but with time I did start to question my own transactional approach to meditation during that first retreat. Like a drop of dye spreading its stain across a whole tapestry, Nisha's suggestion to me over the phone took on more and more meaning. Was I also someone who used meditation solely for my own selfish ends rather than being open to its spiritual foundation?

Maybe she was right. *Just submit yourself to the experience.* By refusing to let go of my own goals and presumptions, perhaps I had robbed myself of – of what?

5

CONFRONTING ANICCA (IMPERMANENCE)

———————❊———————

NISHA had signed me up for my second retreat at a place called Nagarjunasagar, a picturesque town on the banks of the river Krishna. The retreat, like all Vipassana retreats, was spare and modest: there were wooden huts scattered around an enclosed meadow, where we shared rooms with two or three other students.

The programme was designed as an intensive and immersive experience, and students were expected to keep to a rigid schedule. At 4.00 a.m. sharp, an assistant teacher would strike the gong along each dormitory as a wake-up call. By 4:30 a.m., we needed to wash, change and file into the main hall for the first hour of meditation. Each student was provided one pillow and one blanket. The whole class faced the two assistant teachers seated in lotus position at one end of the room.

From early morning until eight in the evening, we had one-hour sittings during which we were instructed on how to meditate. There were short breaks between these sittings. We were given two simple vegetarian meals every day and an hour of walking or light exercise. We had to spend an hour in the evenings listening to the discourses, which were taped videos explaining the practice and history of Vipassana. Phones, newspapers, books, papers and journals (essentially all forms of media) were not allowed, so the hour of discourse was effectively our only external stimulus during the entire ten days of retreat.

Students were also expected to observe 'noble silence' for the entirety of the retreat. Not only did that mean you could not speak to any other student, but it also meant that even acknowledging the presence of others was discouraged. People walked with their gaze directed at the ground, careful not to make eye contact with anyone.

The point was to remove oneself from all external stimuli – including human interaction – to truly quieten the mind. In so much of life we are directed outwards, looking to other people, to media, to books, to tradition, as our source of understanding or knowledge. The aim of meditation is to get one to travel inwards and gain some deeper insight about reality in the here-and-now.

Memories resurfaced and percolated into my conscious mind as I went through the initiation routine. I remembered the sound of the gong from the first retreat, and was reminded of the pain that would shoot through my knees when I stood up after a long session of meditation. There was a familiarity to it; I could still feel a blockage or resistance in my mind, some glass wall that separated me from the other meditators.

The truth was, I did not believe that the spiritual transformation promised by Vipassana was possible. It seemed too obscure and unbound by science to be real.

Yet this time, at Nagarjunasagar, I observed noble silence without secretly exercising or breaking the retreat routine. I followed all of the instructors' rules and practised the technique as I was supposed to. Within a few days my mind began to react strongly to the intense meditative schedule.

A place of pure silence and pure removal is deafening in comparison to the constant stream of communication, information and media of daily life. The occasional birdsong from my dormitory window and the light rain tapping on the roof of the meditation centre were the only two indicators of an external world, and adjusting to this extreme isolation meant that my mind went into overdrive, desperately looking for a release.

During the meditation sittings, my mind raced from thought to thought, memory to memory, anxiety to anxiety, as if it were let loose by the pressure of the silence. I slept only one or two hours every night, and when I did, I had long, complex nightmares that shook me from my half-consciousness. I also began crying for no apparent reason, often opening my eyes after a meditation session or a nap to find my cheeks streaked with tears.

During lunch on the fourth day, I paid a visit to the assistant teacher's hut. I described my worrisome symptoms – the insomnia, the nightmares, the inadvertent crying, the racing mind that was somewhat controlled during meditation but which ricocheted to a heightened, agitated state after each session.

'This is completely normal,' the assistant teacher said with a kind smile. 'Many students mistakenly believe that there is something wrong with them because of these unpleasant experiences. Especially with Noble Silence, since you cannot compare your reactions with others.'

'But everyone else seems so ... *calm.*' I was surprised by the strength of my own exasperation. 'I feel like I'm going crazy. It does make me feel like something is wrong with me.'

'Do not worry. I assure you that this happens quite frequently.'

'When will it end? What is the reason for this?'

'You are trying to clear your mind of impurities, to regain control over the mind. Just like when a wound has been opened, the poison will rise to the surface, so too, as you work to clear your mind, these impurities will rise to the surface. Let them rise, and do not react, and you will find that in time your mind will come back under your control.'

I was not convinced, but Nisha's voice rang in my head again: *Just submit yourself to the experience.*

———

I started looking forward to the taped discourses in the evenings, something that could relieve my information-starved mind after hours of meditation. The discourses were videotaped talks given by S.N. Goenka, the founder of the Vipassana meditation organization. Besides discussing the theory underpinning Vipassana meditation, Goenka shared anecdotes and experiences from his own life.

S.N. Goenka was born in Mandalay, Myanmar, in 1924, as the son of a well-off business family. By his late twenties, Goenka had struck success as a pioneering industrialist. In one of his discourses in the earlier half of the retreat, a smiling Goenka says in his deep, lilting voice that he is glad to have been born into a rich family. 'Otherwise,' he says, his eyes twinkling before the punchline, 'I would have assumed that rich people are happy. I am very lucky that that myth was so quickly dispelled, very lucky.'[1]

With his business success and rising social status, Goenka explained, his ego inflated. He became arrogant and accustomed to everything and everyone in life revolving around his personal needs. It was during this time that he began to suffer severe migraine attacks, each attack leaving him bedridden and tortured. The best doctors in Myanmar could offer no clear diagnosis or treatment; instead they gave him morphine injections after each severe episode.

Fearing debilitation and addiction to morphine, Goenka travelled to many countries in search of a cure. 'I spent a long time in Switzerland, Germany, America, Japan. But I was very fortunate,' he said, again with that twinkling smile. 'No doctor was able to treat me.'

He was faced with dwindling options when his childhood friend suggested Vipassana meditation.

'Vipassana?' Goenka asked. 'What is Vipassana?'

'Meditation,' his friend replied. 'Your disease seems to be psychosomatic, so why not try a technique that is meant to purify the mind?'

Taking his friend's advice to heart, Goenka embarked on his first ten-day Vipassana course in 1956 at the International

Meditation Centre in Rangoon. Upon arrival he met with the meditation teacher, who welcomed him. But when Goenka revealed that his goal was to rid himself of his torturous, chronic migraine attacks, the teacher recoiled and looked at him with a sad expression.

'I am sorry, but now I cannot grant you entry to the retreat,' the teacher said.

'Why? I have applied and have been granted admission like every other student.'

'Dhamma (The Way of the Buddha) is a way of life, not a cure for migraine. By treating dhamma as a cure for your sickness, you are devaluing its worth.'

Recounting this anecdote from his younger days, Goenka explained why he explicitly discouraged his students from attending the retreat with this transactional mindset. Vipassana was not a cure for a specific problem. It was not something that you could truly experience with one narrow goal in mind. *Submit yourself to the experience*, as Nisha said. But now I understood that this 'submitting' meant being open and permeable, not only to learning the technique of Vipassana meditation, but to a way of life and a set of values. In short, one had to be open to an ethical and dispositional transformation.

The only way to *submit to the experience* was to let go of all past paradigms of understanding, including rational and intellectual understanding. Goenka repeated this point often: it was not religion or dogma or science that was at work in Vipassana, but the unnamable experience itself, the physical and mental *presentness* of experience, that would change you. There was no set of rules, or truths. Understanding came through experience, and experience was rooted in the physical and mental practice of the technique itself.

After his first few Vipassana retreats, Goenka decided to leave his past behind, renouncing his businesses, his fame and his identity as an influential industrialist in Burma. Instead, he focused on teaching Vipassana, a practice that had been lost to much of the world (except Burma) due to migration and also destruction of Buddhist texts.

Once an entrepreneur, though, always an entrepreneur. Goenka was not just any practitioner, but the founder of the Vipassana institute, whose mission has been to restore the practice by setting up free meditation centres across the world. Every year, the organization holds 1,000 courses in over ninety countries across the world. There are Vipassana meditation programmes in even prisons and schools. The organization is entirely donation-funded and volunteer-run. Every course and retreat is run by previous students and assistant teachers, who 'give back' by 'serving', for no financial reward. Under this entirely charitable model, the Vipassana organization has survived and grown over the decades.

Goenka rarely appealed to faith (the basis of religious affiliation) or rational truth (the basis of intellectual affiliation) in any of his discourses. 'The results will speak for themselves,' he would repeat again and again. 'If this technique has a good effect on your life, then you will not need faith or intellect to justify it.'

In retrospect, even if there were no other benefits to be obtained from the retreat, it would have been worth it to return for a Vipassana course simply for the chance to listen to Goenkaji. One of his students rightfully describes him as a man 'shining with compassion' – that twinkle in his smile while he recounts anecdotes of his misguided past radiates with kindness, forgiveness, empathy.

Whether it was his entrepreneurial mindset, his personal history or his compassionate exuberance, projecting a sense of enlightened humility even across grainy video projection, I felt he was someone who could help me answer some of the questions that had accumulated in my mind since my time in the ICU. With each passing day I listened with more concentration, in search of some grain of truth that would resonate with my search for a new mode of being.

———

For me, Vipassana was a radical transformation of insight. If the years I took off from business were a pause, then Vipassana was the beginning of a new beginning, a path that revealed itself after many years of my wandering.

The word 'Vipassana' has two components – 'passana', which means sight or perception, and 'vi', which means deep or powerful, the act of passing through. 'Vipassana,' in short, is a meditative practice that promotes experiential insight, so that you can *see through* delusions or misunderstandings of the mind.

The technique of Vipassana meditation works within the framework of the individual body.[2] You are instructed to focus on the sensations in your body and mind, without reacting favourably to 'good' sensations (pleasant tingling, warmth, happy thoughts) or unfavourably to 'bad' sensations (itches, aches, pains, unhappy thoughts).

'Maintain perfect equanimity, perfect equanimity.' Do not allow the mind to react, even infinitesimally, to any perceived pleasure or pain. Hours pass, and students are immersed in a state of intense focus and awareness of their body and mind, and of the rising and passing away of innumerable sensations previously unnoticed.

My mind started acclimatizing to the practice, and I found that outside of meditating hours my thought processes were clearer, and that I was more calm. I could think about my past, present and future with a clarity that I never felt before. But beyond these changes, which I had felt during my first retreat too, another strange feeling began to set in – the sensation that I was smaller and smaller, that my individual dreams and fantasies were dwarfed by the vastness of the cosmos.

At night, when I could not sleep, I would leave my dormitory and sit outside. The night sky above Nagarjunasagar was free from pollution, free from the light remnants that lingered over cities. The stars were the brightest that I had ever seen.

At Nagarjunasagar, I was undergoing, for the first time in my life, a decentring of the ego. This was an immensely counterintuitive experience. Although the Vipassana practice required intense immersion within and awareness of oneself as an individual unit of mankind, the technique actually dissolved and reconstructed my identity as an 'individual' in the traditional sense.

Here, the Buddhist concept of *anicca* (pronounced 'anichya') is crucial. As one of the three core 'insights' that Vipassana meditation is meant to reveal, anicca means impermanence and continual change. During Vipassana, by isolating yourself from all external stimuli and focusing on your mind and body, you begin to *experience* the reality of this impermanence – not in thought, but in visceral understanding. Every single sensation that you feel and every single thought that surfaces in the mind then shares this quality of impermanence and change.

In the mind's regular, everyday state, its rhythm and conditioning instinctively reacts to various physical or mental feelings. You shift your position to stretch out a cramp, or scratch the back of the neck to rid yourself of the creeping itch, or you feel happy or unhappy based on the content of your thoughts, flitting from future fantasy to past regret. The point of meditation is *not* to react to these feelings but to observe them and maintain a perfect stillness of mind and body.

With practice, you notice that the pain bothering you in your leg fades after fifteen minutes. The itching sensation behind your ear becomes more intense before it disappears without your needing to scratch it. Your broodings about the past and your wandering daydreams about the future are dispelled as you bring your mind back into focus. You feel physical sensations and your mental drift rise and fall. The one thing that threads them together is that they are all impermanent and constantly changing. Every sensation or thought is defined by this process of arriving and passing away, rising and falling, ebbing and flowing.

You may ask how this relates to the ego. The truth is that I still cannot fully understand or explain this phenomenon, but through meditation I began to register anicca at the experiential level. In routine life the mind is not accustomed to staying attuned with the tiny, momentary changes and evidence of impermanence in our body and brain. This lack of awareness means that, on some abstract level, we begin to believe in the idea of ourselves as permanent, stable and continual beings; the construction of the ego is essentially an attachment to and identification with that seemingly stable entity.

By meditating, awareness of anicca rises to the surface, and the infinitesimal variations in physical and mental sensations begin to reveal a deeper truth about your own self. By bringing your mind to a state of meditative awareness, you start to realize that the basic fundamental truth about the 'self' is that it is made up of a constantly evolving flurry of physical and mental sensations, little blips that vanish as quickly as they emerge.

For the meditator, this experiential truth can be abstracted to the concept of the self. Qualities that you feel trapped by, that you see as merged with your own 'self', such as anxiety, fear and arrogance, are not essential elements of your ego, but simply *objects* of awareness that can be observed and discarded, just like the sensations which rise and fall in your body and brain. Similarly, qualities that you are proud of and identify with, such as courage or passion, are also objects of awareness, and thereby vulnerable to change. Meditation, by directing awareness to the transitory and impermanent nature of our self-representation, reveals this *deconstruction* of the self and ego.

Something that begins with a task as basic as paying attention to one's body and breath suddenly creates ripples through the mind, revealing previously dormant insights into the true nature of the self. We are not stable, continuous selves. We are each a process, a flow of impermanent sensations. 'Anicca, anicca, anicca.'

This was the chant that concluded every meditation session, and the ultimate reminder from the retreat that I carried with me.

I tried to understand how – beyond the experiential level, which in and of itself entails no intellectual or rational comprehension – this insight could figure in my daily life. What did it mean that elements we so closely tie to the 'self' (thoughts, feelings, physical characteristics) were not, in reality, continual or unchanging? What could I do with this new understanding, that impermanence and continual change made up the true nature of my being? What were the implications of this?

The Buddhist tradition posits that the idea of a stable, continual self is not a neutral or innocent belief. On the contrary, the attachment to this idea of a concrete, continual self is a strong and dangerous source of unhappiness.[3] The worst vices or unethical tendencies – greed (unnatural attachment) and aversion (ill-will towards objects, feelings or other people) – are born out of egoism and the *misunderstanding* of the self as a necessary, unchanging essence.

One of Goenka's stories explains how belief in this central ego creates unhappiness. In the story, Goenka and his students are walking near a river. One of the students accidentally trips over a man sleeping by the riverbank. The man awakens, and angrily shouts, 'What are you doing? Do you have eyes or buttonholes?' When this happens, Goenka experiences a pleasant feeling.

The next day, Goenka is walking alone by the river when he accidentally trips over a man sleeping by the riverbank. The man wakes up and angrily shouts, 'What are you doing? Do you have eyes or buttonholes?' When this happens, Goenka experiences an unpleasant feeling.

The next day, Goenka is again walking along the riverbank with his students, and again trips over a sleeping man. The man shouts, 'What are you doing? Do you have eyes or buttonholes?' When this happens, Goenka experiences an even more unpleasant feeling.

On the fourth day, Goenka is again on the same walk with his students and he accidentally trips over a man sleeping by the riverbank. The man wakes up and shouts, 'What are you doing? Do you have eyes or buttonholes?' The man now approaches

Goenka, and the teacher realizes that the man sleeping by the riverbank is his own son. When this happens, Goenka experiences an extremely unpleasant feeling.

In each of these instances, the same harm has been done to the universe, the same mistake made, and the same pain inflicted on the man by the riverbank. Yet Goenka's unhappiness is determined not by the objective damage done to the universe, but by the reactions of his own ego. In the first instance, Goenka was pleased because his ego or self-image of being a mentor to his naïve, clumsy students was affirmed. He was not the one to make the mistake, to create harm in the world. This resulted in a pleasant feeling. In the second instance, Goenka was upset because his self-image as a faultless teacher was attacked. Next, he felt even more unhappy when his students witnessed his mistake, for his ego and self-image were then subjected to the judgement of others. Lastly, the unhappiness was made *even* worse when the homeless man by the river was discovered to be his son, who is connected to Goenka's own sense of self. *Oh no*, he thinks. *Now my students have seen me, the faultless teacher, make a mistake* and *fail my own son*. In all four instances, the ego determined and distorted the reaction.

Meditation as a practice is meant to help quieten and control the mind so that it is possible to *detach* oneself from the distress of clinging to an egocentric self-representation, to cut through the delusion of the ego.

In the positive sense, this decentring of the ego allows for the beneficial identification with those besides ourselves, motivating in us a sense of compassion for all beings. Indeed, the radical insight of non-self is not to close the door to one's egocentrism, but to open the possibility for a life of empathy and connectivity. It is the message that all harm in the world is harm, even to those distant and unfamiliar to us, *in spite of* who 'we' are. It is spiritual openness rather than rational isolation; it is reaching out with one's hand rather than clutching on to individual possession; it is a holistic way of life rather than a modular mode of being. In this sense, within the broader ethical framework of meditation, experiencing and understanding non-egocentrism is perhaps most importantly a means of acquiring the ability to be constantly and justly compassionate.

As Goenka described the unbearable tensions in his life prior to his learning meditation, I realized that this fixation on the ego had been the root of much of my own unhappiness too. The obsessional attitude towards my businesses, the growing animosity in my personal relationships and the dwindling sense of meaning in life, seemed to have all derived from an egoistic hubris that left me disconnected from others and from any sense of purpose.

Even my reflections in the ICU now seemed incomplete, as I was only concerned with my own personal development as an entrepreneur. I was not open to compassion, or to a perspective with a more collective purpose in mind. I was still clinging to my own sense of self, my mission, my individual identity.

Whereas in Nagarjunasagar, I was nobody – I was merely one amongst many, and that 'I', too, was impermanent, a fragment nestled within the interminable change and renewal that is life in its truest form.

———

There is something very challenging about this experience of the decentring of one's ego. Some people even say that deep immersion in meditative practices is not possible in normal everyday life because you cannot go through daily life without an ego. Unless you dedicate yourself to the seclusion of a teacher or a monk, these critics argue, meditation is unhelpful or even detrimental, since functioning in the 'real world' *demands* action, stimulus and operating with a unique sense of self. It is as if meditating could destroy this ability and leave the meditator unable to survive in society. I understood these concerns as one of my own many irrational fears, when I first learned about the practice, that meditation would dull my ambitions, erase my identity and somehow change me into a hermit.

However, the decentring of one's ego is *not* some irreversible destruction of all identity or sense of self-interest. During the retreat, I did not even once feel a sense of loss or self-destruction. Instead, by setting aside my ego, I could see through a new window of truth, which showed the ego for what it was.

This window revealed the self not as a concrete truth, but as a convenient construction that we should not latch on to too tightly. In the moments we make serious decisions or reflect on the greater meaning of our lives, we can peer into this window for the understanding that attachment to our ego-construction can distort our thinking and bring unhappiness in terms of attachment, greed or aversion.

Ultimately, the aim of meditation is not obliteration of the individual unit for the collective. Other species, such as ants, may operate on an entirely collective principle, their actions dictated by algorithmic processes prioritizing species and genus over the individual. Ant colonies *do* obliterate individual ant identity, becoming 'superorganisms' of collective consciousness, as opposed to the constituents operating as discrete individual units.

Meditative practice, on the other hand, does not destroy the self to the point of disintegration. Rather, it decentres the ego and reveals its true nature. By doing this, the narrow focus we place on the self dissolves, and our mind opens to the idea of a broader collective perspective, that of the 'many', as opposed to the ever-changing 'I'.

There is some truth to the tension that many critics point to – a kind of unresolved disconnect between the meditative state and everyday life. As a layperson (householder) who practises meditation, the moment you leave the retreat is when this tension, or cognitive dissonance, begins to set in. In psychology, cognitive dissonance is the discomfort experienced by someone who simultaneously holds two or more conflicting beliefs, ideas or values in her mind. In philosophy, the existence of two such beliefs, ideas or values is known as contradiction.

Leaving the retreat triggers this deep sense of cognitive dissonance. You are no longer sheltered within the isolation and quietude of the retreat, where it is natural to cultivate a serene, contemplative state. You are withdrawn from the external world, in a sense. Yet outside the retreat, in the 'real' world of obligations, family, chores and livelihoods, it is often impossible to be in the same mindset. In some cases, it may even be detrimental to be so. Suddenly, the ethos and passivity of the retreat clash with the demands of modern reality and daily life.

The cognitive dissonance extends even further to strike at the very tension between the ego and the connectivity of beings: Self versus Other, Individual versus Community. While the ego is displaced, you understand the importance of working with the collective in mind, with some identification with a larger purpose or scope of life. Yet, in life, the ego is also necessary for everyday decision-making, and is instrumental in forming a basis for motivation and action.

I have been wrestling with this question for some time now, as have thinkers and writers far more knowledgeable and insightful than I will ever be. My view is that, rather than seeing this cognitive dissonance as an obstacle to be confronted or a problem to be resolved, perhaps this core contradiction is, in fact, a necessary part of productive reflection. It is not something to run away from, despite the discomfort it induces – but something to embrace.

I have always loved this F. Scott Fitzgerald quote: 'The test of a first-rate intelligence is the ability to hold two opposed ideas in mind at the same time and still retain the ability to function.'

The key is to find some way to hold the sets of opposing objectives intact – personal well-being and collective interest, the equanimity of meditation and the action of reality, a sense of self and an impersonal ethical position – while retaining one's ability to function in the world.

———

The echo of this cognitive dissonance has resounded throughout history and in all religions and literature. I believe this is because of its central role in our human condition. In the Bhagavad Gita, Krishna presents this dictum to a beloved warrior: *Be in the world, but not of the world.* Perhaps this same message has been part of so many religious texts because the cognitive dissonance between Self and All is at the heart of religion's chief purpose: to understand what it means to be a good or ethical human being.

An ethical position is, essentially, an impersonal standpoint concerned with the welfare of others. The position of ethical consideration changes our perspective from that of an inward-facing eye to that of something vastly abstracted. To think from an ethical position, one must admit: 'I am one of many, and I am one part of an eternal continuum.' Yet this impersonal standpoint, concerned with the welfare of others, clashes with one's individual self-interest, that 'inward-facing eye' we use to perceive and act in daily life.

The point I am trying to make is that this cognitive dissonance, although it does produce some discomfort or uncertainty, is central to the human process of formulating meaning and morality. We should not run away from the discomfort, but accept it as part of the tension that makes life difficult, yet meaningful. *Be in the world, but not of the world.*

Vipassana taught me how to be *not of the world.* Now I had a technique that could, with continual practice, bring me back to that detached, clear-headed and compassionate perspective. This opened a completely new understanding of reality, and of what is valuable in life. I saw that my existence could no longer be organized solely for a narrow set of goals that I had constructed for my ego, but that it was connected and purposeful in relation to all beings.

In the ICU, I had the thought that I was entering a second life, but it was not until I left Nagarjunasagar that I comprehended what this would mean. It was, at last, the start of a new beginning.

6

A CHANGED MAN

———✳———

MY radical insight from Vipassana gave me a new set of eyes. I left the retreat with a surreal lightness, as if I had shed a weight that I did not know existed. As I drove back into Hyderabad, I looked out of the window at the passing fields, trying to etch the feeling of that lightness in my memory.

I felt peacefully disassociated from myself, watching the outside world from a new and nameless place. When the mind is unclouded, when it does not have to sift through a chorus of conflicting voices, decisions that were once impossible become clear. Upon leaving the retreat I had reached three conclusions. They were thoughts that surfaced during the retreat and struck a chord in my mind.

Firstly, I knew I was ready to return to work, to start a business again. I did not know what business, or how I would start it, but I knew that I would build something in the next few years. The paralysis I had experienced was broken by Vipassana, which gifted me the insight of being connected to the value of all that is beyond the individual self. Secondly, I was ready to settle down and live somewhere permanently. Returning to Hyderabad was exactly what I needed for a few years, but I also needed some distance from the trappings of the past. That was why I had left for Mumbai in my twenties – to force myself into independence and unfamiliarity.

Lastly, I was ready to face the truth about the person who occupied my mind and my dreams throughout the retreat: Helen, the woman whom I had mentioned to Nisha, the woman I was growing to love. I had met Helen a few months ago while climbing Mount Kiliminjaro. She was part of the eight-person cohort making the trek, and we spent ten continuous days exchanging snippets of conversation as we scaled the mountain. By the end of the trip I had already grown attached to her strength and witty sense of humour.

I dialled Helen's number in the car as we were nearing Hyderabad.

'I'm coming to San Francisco,' was the only thing I said into the phone, and she understood.

When I arrived at Helen's apartment, she welcomed me into her living room. From her large living room window, you could see the glittering facade of Bay Bridge. Helen looked lovely, her skin glowing and her smile radiant. I entered and hugged her close to me.

'You're back,' she said softly.

'Of course,' I said.

'There is no fixed course for anything, Ravi.' And she was right. We had never established what our relationship would be in the future, never made that commitment aloud.

Helen got up and made a cup of black tea for me and fetched water for herself. She was eager to hear about the meditation retreat.

'It was a complete overturning,' I began. 'You sit there all day, every day, with absolutely nothing to distract you. I don't know how, but something in the wiring of your brain changes. I could *feel* it.' I told her about the discomfort, the nightmares, the crying and, finally, the decentring of ego that led to a wave of acceptance and peace.

She took it all in, stopping to ask a few questions now and then. I was relieved. Before I arrived I was worried that Helen, who was a scientist through and through, might laugh off meditation as some sort of hack.

'What do you think this means? In the grand scheme of things?' she finally asked.

'I'm not sure,' I replied. 'It's certainly allowed me to think more clearly about the exact root of my problems. For a long time, my life no longer had meaning, because I had lost touch with a greater purpose. I was only concerned with myself – *my* reputation as an entrepreneur, *my* businesses, *my* tangential solutions. I sacrificed everything for that.'

'And now?'

'Now I understand that those things will never bring me any lasting fulfilment.'

'Do you think you will ever go back to being an entrepreneur?'

'I think I am ready to.'

Helen raised her eyebrows.

'Let me explain. When I first moved to Mumbai, I was such an idealist. I thought starting a business was like solving a puzzle or a theoretical math problem. If you thought hard enough, you would eventually find an elegant solution in the ether.'

'Your first few years in Mumbai must have proved otherwise.' We both chuckled. Mumbai was such a chaotic place; of course, it clashed with the ideals I had dreamt up in Golconda.

'Definitely a shock of realism', I replied. 'My father had warned me that entrepreneurship was messy and real, not just a mental game, but I always thought his views had to do with his generation, or his particular industries. I thought I could avoid the chaos and messiness that I saw in his businesses by making decisions different from his.'

'But you were unable to do that, and your idealism was shattered, to some extent.'

'Exactly. I was thoroughly unprepared for the harsh aspects of business, the morally questionable aspects. I was also shy, aloof – a person who lived in his own head. I did not understand why everyone was chasing after wealth and power. I just wanted to build businesses like I wanted to solve puzzles, or hike.'

'I remember one banker in New York,' I continued, 'who leaned over after we had signed a deal, and said, "My bonus depends on how much I'm screwing your happiness." He was smirking! I honestly do not know what disturbed me more – that he openly admitted to being incentivized to work against my happiness, or that he believed my happiness was directly proportional to the amount of money I would make.' I shook my head in disbelief, remembering the shock I had felt at what he had said. I was just a kid then.

'And I did nothing to challenge this, Helen. I became so easily *complicit*, and absorbed by the system. When I arrived in Mumbai, I did not have a good understanding of the world I was living in, but before I even fully understood it, I was a part of it. Not only did I become a *part* of it, I sacrificed so much for it, including my family. Once you are caught up in the rat-race, it's incredibly difficult to disentangle yourself. '

'Why do you think that is?'

'During meditation, this is what I realized. For the past five years, I thought that the problem was my work–life balance. If I organized my business differently, or my role, and dedicated some time to other pursuits, everything would be resolved.'

'What is wrong with that?'

'That's the thing I learned from meditation. I will *never* find fulfilment or peace by optimizing work–life balance, or by tweaking my businesses. I was making the wrong diagnosis all along.'

She looked confused, but I continued. 'During Vipassana, I kept returning to the *root* of unhappiness. Everything that appeared to be a problem was a symptom. The real root of my unhappiness, the cause of it, was that by giving in to my ego, I lost touch with my principles and purpose. I lost touch with the spiritual understanding of myself as an impermanent being. I loved the process of building businesses, but I failed to reflect on its fundamental value. Everything I built was built with ego – my idea of entrepreneurship, my success, my solutions.

'*Why were these businesses valuable to me*? was not the right question. I should have been asking – *how were these businesses valuable to others?* To those whom I loved? To other beings on Earth? What principles would I follow, not only in entrepreneurship, but in anything I did in life, that would ensure I was dedicating my time and energy to something valuable beyond my own self?

'I always thought the value of a business was measured by its technical elegance, as in how intelligently it was set up, or how creatively it was structured, or how much it grew in a period. But the value of a business should really be measured by how it is able to generate value for a greater collective – for the greater good. And this does not apply to just your business, but to anything you do in life.

'You see, I realized that without a greater purpose, without an understanding of how we are interrelated to others and how our own lives can produce real value for those far beyond ourselves, any passion, including entrepreneurship, becomes an empty shell. Even if we refuse to admit it, a part of us understands that our individual lives are impermanent. Many try to fight that impermanence by accumulating material things, status, whatever, thinking they can be made immortal by satisfying the ego and attaching it to all sorts of worldly possessions. I met so many unhappy people in Mumbai who were like that.'

'Well, what's the alternative?'

'The alternative is to understand and embrace the impermanence, and let go of the ego. The ego is like Sisyphus. Every time we carry the boulder up the mountain, it rolls back down again, demanding more effort and enslaving us to its wishes. Letting that go opens a whole world of possibilities, where you are connected to others and your actions aim to create value for all life. You will not believe how liberating that is.'

Helen looked at me with a confused but kind expression. I knew she was having trouble absorbing everything that I had said. 'Helen,' I finally said. 'I feel like I have the answers to build a new life. These past five years have been like one extended dream, but I am ready to build a new life, with purpose. With you.'

Her eyes widened, then she looked down with a pained expression. 'But you are going to go back to India,' she said, almost in a whisper. 'We both just got divorced; we didn't expect to meet each other or fall in love. I bet you are thinking of building a new business already. Our lives are so complicated ... how will we ever make it work?'

I asked her to trust me. I would not make the same mistake twice. To start from a decentred perspective meant that I would overhaul my entire process of entrepreneurship and life-building.

In the past, I started with the business and moulded my life to its development, whatever the cost. This time I would do the reverse: start with the people I loved, then with the purpose I would define, and then build a life and business that moulded to these factors.

I knew where I wanted to be. I just needed to figure out how to get there.

––––

In San Francisco, Helen and I began each morning with a walk on the Embarcadero, the boardwalk just beneath Oakland Bay Bridge. The wind was usually brisk, and the reflection of the waterfront skyscrapers was like a distorted metal playground rippling in the waves. I held Helen's hand in the breeze, silently reminding myself never to forget the preciousness of these moments. *I must cherish this feeling, this bliss between us,* I thought to myself.

My promise to Helen was that I would not make the same mistakes I had in the past. I would not lose myself in my goals at the expense of others. Decentring required inverting the interpersonal and the personal, building a life that prioritized, as its unchangeable premise, the happiness and well-being of others.

Although the intention was sound, keeping this promise was not easy. I was forty-two, and had spent the past five years in an uncertain limbo. In fact, Helen and I were *both* going through transitions that allowed for a sort of flexible, nomadic wandering, but our core lives were scattered across the world. My network of family and friends, previous businesses and, most importantly, children, were all in India, whereas she had called San Francisco and Boston home for the past thirty years. I wanted to start another business, and she wanted to travel the world after a long professional career.

We decided to move to a place where neither of us had any roots – a clean slate for our new life. A few months later, we found an apartment in Fulham, a leafy residential neighbourhood in south-west London. We moved into a refurbished building that was once the headquarters of British Gas. The apartment was quirky and perfect. The building was right next to a public park, and from our balcony we could see the dark waters of the Thames streaming along.

The one thing that unsettled me about this new life was its distance from my children, Daman and Aditi. My divorce process was a long one, and took a visible toll on my entire family, especially the kids. Within my family, and in India more generally, divorce was still very much stigmatized, and I found that most of my family were in active opposition to it. By the time the terms of the divorce were finalized, a sense of defeat settled in. I still remember leaving the court in Chennai, a dim box of a building painted the colour of burnt potato skin.

Alone, I muscled past the crowd gathered outside, putting my hand over my face in case I wept.

As it is in most divorces, the mother was granted custody – I had never doubted Charita's love or care for the children, and so I agreed with the arrangements. Helen and I took care to be as involved in their lives as was possible. Charita too thawed after the finalization of the divorce, and we established an amicable routine.

One winter, the children visited Helen and me in London for their Christmas break. Daman was nearly eight at the time, and my daughter Aditi was six. A few days passed and we were having a relaxed time hanging out as a family. We took pictures at the Tower Bridge, bought gingerbread cookies and hot chocolate at the Christmas market in Trafalgar Square and watched movies at home. Since this trip was longer than their usual visits, Helen constructed a study schedule for the kids. She wagged her fingers at them when their eyes widened; they had had their fun, but there would be some work to do too.

The next morning Helen came up to me in the living room. 'Ravi, I have something to tell you.' The distress in her tone made my heart sink into my stomach feel like a heavy pit.

'What is it? Is something wrong?'

'I don't know … I think so.' She was chewing the inside of her lip. I had never seen Helen at a loss for words before.

'What is it, sweetie? Just tell me.'

'It's Daman.' She sighed, then quickly looked around to make sure we were alone. 'I told him and Aditi yesterday that we would start reading half an hour a day together. Just some basic reading to get them ready for their term at school. So, I went to Daman's room, and we picked a book together from his English class.' She leaned in close to me. 'Ravi, I think there is something wrong.'

'What do you mean?'

'Daman … he cannot read. He was stumbling and having trouble with the sentences on the page. He squinted the whole time and was not be able to sound out most of the words.'

She paused, as if readying me for what she was about to say. 'Ravi, my dad was a high school teacher who worked with children with disabilities. I know what the signs are.'

'The signs of what, exactly?'

'I think Daman is seriously dyslexic. We need to do something as soon as we can if we want to keep his development on track.'

I sat down and steadied myself. This was my son, the light of my life. Her words were pounding in my heart. I could hardly believe what I was hearing. If this were true, then his entire education may be compromised. How did we not discover this until now?

'It happens, Ravi.' It was as if Helen could hear my very thoughts. 'They do not have the resources for learning disabilities in Chennai. Charita must have thought he was just falling behind because of your divorce and all the changes in his young life, which is completely understandable. We spent time with him, but always on vacation. There was really no way to know. These things are hard to identify.'

I still found it difficult to speak. Only in these moments, when the unexpected hurls you into uncertainty, does the peaceful past stand in sharp contrast. But I needed to ready myself to do something, anything, to help Daman.

We wasted no time in taking action. That very evening Helen took Daman to a local education expert who recommended a comprehensive four-hour learning abilities test. I still remember holding Daman's hand before he entered the test room alone. He was trying so hard to be strong, hiding the fear that showed only in the corners of his eyes, that it almost broke my heart.

The results of the tests showed that Daman was on the severe side of the dyslexic spectrum, with a possible non-verbal learning disorder. The consultant recommended immediate intervention.

Over the next few months, I researched academies with special services for learning disabilities in Chennai, Singapore, the US and London. Charita and I visited these schools together, consulted experts, and debated the best course of action. There were simply not enough high-quality schools suitable for Daman's condition in India, but it would also be difficult for Charita to leave Chennai, where her entire extended family and support system was based.

'Ravi, listen to me.' Helen and I were visiting a school in Boston, which had a personalized learning programme for children with dyslexia, when she stopped in the hallway. 'Why don't we think about gaining custody?'

'I've thought about it,' I admitted. 'Many times. I just do not know if Charita would agree with it. We need to focus on what is best for the children.'

'Exactly, Ravi. What is best for the children. There is no way they will receive the same resources in India. We have to take them to either the UK or the US, that much has become clear.'

She was right. 'But we are going to have to radically change the way this family is set up, Helen. We will be the primary caregivers of the children. Are you ready for that?' Helen never had any children of her own, and this was an unexpected and massive responsibility.

'Ravi, I don't care. I am ready. If you …' She jabbed my chest with her index finger, 'and I have been blessed with such wonderful education, there is no way in hell (she said it as if in four separate sentences: No. Way. In. Hell.) I'm going to let your son miss out on the same.' She insisted that we push for custody or relocate Charita to England so we could jointly care for the children. In my heart, I was already thinking the same, and felt a rush of relief that she agreed.

After negotiating with Charita for months, we rewrote the terms of our divorce and transferred primary custody of the children to me. For my part, I was also incredibly lucky to have two adaptable, strong children, who took all these changes in their stride. Daman, especially, was resolute and calm throughout the whole process. He has always been a boy with an unimaginably kind heart.

'I would not have believed this five years ago, Ravi,' I remember Charita saying to me. She still remembered me as an absentee husband and father. 'You're a changed man.'

———

In many ways I did feel like a changed man. The bond between myself and those whom I loved had strengthened significantly. With Vipassana, the uncertainty and the searching that had clouded the past five years had also lifted. I felt ready, finally, to restart my life.

But I knew I would not be the same kind of entrepreneur that I was before. In the past I had been immensely proud of my tangential solutions. They were like puzzles that I pondered over, attempted and eventually solved. By thinking about entrepreneurship as an art form I had unknowingly assumed that the purpose of entrepreneurship was self-expression. I was the artist, and the business was my canvas. I had never reflected on what real value my businesses created. To me, the tangential solution was what was important. It did not matter if the business created payphones for the poor like Zip or if it simply turned out a significant profit by exploiting a contractual opportunity like Altius.

After Vipassana, this philosophy and method of entrepreneurship no longer seemed sufficient. I could no longer work without considering how my businesses would impact a bigger collective of human lives and their well-being beyond the narrow range of my companies. I could no longer live in my isolated mental fantasy of entrepreneurship, a fantasy that never questioned whether what I was doing was actually valuable.

I recently read a novel in which one of the characters, Sebastian, explains the concept of the *maarr*. Tibetan monks wrote about the maarr as a collection of secret wants and needs that form a circle of energy stored in your body. Here, Sebastian describes what it means to see someone else's maarr:

> To 'see' someone's *maarr* means recognizing someone else's desire – without asking, without being told – and acting on it. That last part is essential: the 'seeing' is not complete until one *does something about it*. So, a man only 'sees' a woman's desires when he fulfills them without being asked to do so. A woman 'sees' a hungry man's *maarr* when, unprompted, she gives him food.[1]

It is this *active* sense of empathy I needed to build on. I knew my family's *maarr,* and I could catch glimpses of society's *maarr* too, but I had yet to act on it. Tangential solutions and my previous model of entrepreneurship would not help me in that quest.

What would help me is a myth.

Part II

MYTH OF THE ENTREPRENEUR

And from where you see it, the thing is a whole, the earth is a whole, and it's so beautiful. You wish you could take a person in each hand, one from each side in the various conflicts, and say, 'Look. Look at it from this perspective. Look at that. What's important?'

—Russell Schweickart, *astronaut*

Fᴿᴼᴹ a vehicle in space, you orbit the Earth every few hours – waking up over one continent and eating breakfast over another. The blue and white sphere below, pulsing with the entire range of life as you know it, would look small indeed against the backdrop of black, infinite space. Russell Schweickart, a NASA astronaut, writes beautifully about this in a piece titled 'No Frames, No Boundaries'[1], where he talks about confronting the majesty and profoundness of the scale of our precious Earth juxtaposed against space, and how that perspective opens an active identification with all life:

> And you think about what you're experiencing and why. Do you deserve this? Have you earned this in some way? Are you separated out to be touched by God, to have some special experience that others cannot have? And you know the answer to that is no …
>
> You are up there *as the sensing element*, that point out on the end, and that's a humbling feeling. It's a feeling that says you have a responsibility. It's not for yourself. The eye that doesn't see doesn't do justice to the body. That's why it's there. That's why you are out there. And somehow you recognize that you're a piece of this total life.

And somehow you recognize that you're a piece of this total life. Leaving Vipassana, I felt in touch, for the first time, with this total life, which shifted the very essence of the way I understood value. And if you will bear with me, dear reader, even though I have taken you on quite the wandering path already, I want to spend the rest of this book telling two stories about how my own change in perspective led me down a wholly new path.

The first story is an archetype – it is the tale of the Entrepreneur with a capital 'E,' and about how we envision this ideal, successful Entrepreneur's place in our world. I construct this 'myth' in order to point out its flaws, in effect breaking my preconceived notion of what an entrepreneur ought to be, and showing how this myth supports a kind of entrepreneurial philosophy that is not conducive to maximal value-creation. The second story is about the entrepreneur with a lower-case 'e,'; it is the actual story of how I built my last company, incorporating the decentring experience of Vipassana and my new understanding of value creation into my enterprise.

When I first began writing this book I wanted to write only about the Entrepreneur with the capital E. It seemed arrogant and selfish – not to mention against my very personality – to publicize my own personal narrative, the story of the entrepreneur with the lower-case 'e'. But friends and family, as well as professors and writers I knew, gradually convinced me that the personal is what makes the universal seem close, accessible, meaningful.

People like to hear stories, not arguments, for a reason. For it is the trickle of water that becomes a river, it is a grain of sand that gives life to a pearl. That is what I want my personal story to be in this book: a grain of sand that disappears as it becomes a small, invisible part of the pearl.

———

Back in my youth, during my days of reading at Golconda, I came across the writings of Thomas Carlyle, a nineteenth-century Scottish philosopher who penned fascinating stories about people like Napoleon, Shakespeare and Frederick the Great. Carlyle's focus on heroic figures was deliberate; he was a major proponent of the Great Man Theory of History, the idea that the arc of human history can be explained by the impact of highly influential individuals possessing qualities like intelligence, political acumen, charisma and strength. As Carlyle summed it up pithily, 'History is but the biography of great men.' (Unfortunately, thinkers such as Carlyle were not yet enlightened enough to pay attention to the other, that is, female half of human population.)

This way of thinking about history has been largely discredited by historians, and for good reason, but I believe many people (myself included) are still inclined to see history as a story driven by a few outliers with major influence. After all, individual heroes and their legacies are more easily understood than the subtle, underlying currents of history. Although the incremental changes in social, economic and political organization may be the true deciding factors of history, they are often difficult to pinpoint and to understand, requiring decades of hindsight. The life of a famous explorer or king and his impact, on the other hand, is direct and observable, not to mention entertaining.

In this day and age, successful entrepreneurs have become some of the most powerful and well-known individual 'movers' of history, the great men and women whose stories people look up to and refer to when they are trying to understand the times in which they live.

Indeed, the personalities of some entrepreneurs command enormous attention and influence in our society. Think Steve Jobs, Elon Musk or Oprah Winfrey in America; Carlos Slim in Mexico; or Mukesh Ambani and Azim Premji in India: these are larger-than-life celebrities who wield the power to shape public consciousness. Of course, there are other influential history-making figures, such as heads of states, religious figures, financiers and artists. Yet none of us can deny that those who founded and created successful ventures of their own now enjoy incredible public renown and influence.

The Myth of the Entrepreneur is very much about how this figure of the 'entrepreneur' has been dominating public imagination as the *rightful* shapers of history and distributors of value. In a world of declining trust in traditional institutions, surveys show that people are looking to entrepreneurs to fuel change. Global PR firm Edelman's annual 'Trust Survey' states that, in 2017, trust in media, government and NGOs declined, with two-thirds of the countries surveyed reporting less than 50 per cent trust in all institutions.[2] Taking advantage of public frustration with traditional politics, the celebrity-entrepreneur Donald Trump has convinced a portion of his country that his talent as an entrepreneur could 'make America great again'. In China too, where businessmen were traditionally viewed as the least respected community in society, 'entrepreneur worship' has taken hold in the midst of the country's unprecedented creation of wealth.[3] Entrepreneurs, it seems, are the only leaders that society is now willing to trust.

The startup culture that grew out of the Internet age accelerated, or even created, this new era of entrepreneur worship. For the first time in the world's history, scrappy young dropouts with a love for technology built an ecosystem of like-minded peers, funding and other resources that allowed for unprecedented creation of wealth, power and innovation. The Entrepreneur is featured at the core of this ecosystem, as a creator of value and a mover of history.

Silicon Valley, as the geographic and ideological centre of this new entrepreneurial age, branded itself as the place where young visionaries came to change the world, so much so that 'changing the world' has become a kind of joke. In the HBO TV show, *Silicon Valley*, every single entrepreneur ends his or her pitch with some grand statement about 'changing the world', even if the project in question is software whose only function is determining whether or not something is a hot dog.[4]

For much of my life I believed in this view of the world, and I worshipped the individual entrepreneur. My bookshelf at home was cluttered with the biographies of 'heroic' figures. But I have come to believe that this glorification of the entrepreneur has been supported by a collection of assumptions, ideas and values that shroud these individual stories into a shared myth of the entrepreneur. By calling it a myth, I am also pointing to the methodology with which we should examine this tale. Myths are a kind of narrative reflecting the cultural values of the myth-creating society. Just as historians analyse the myths of the ancient world to reveal the world view of past societies, I believe it will be a useful exercise to understand and question the myth of the entrepreneur too, in order to reveal aspects of our present-day world view.

An important caveat is that my critique of the myth of the entrepreneur is not a 'profile' of any specific entrepreneur. At the same time, the myth of the entrepreneur does not apply to *many* entrepreneurs, especially small-to-medium-sized business owners, early-stage entrepreneurs, and the countless entrepreneurs who take significant risks every day to deal with struggling ventures. The myth of the entrepreneur, in the context of my analysis, should be seen as pertaining to the entrepreneur who is, in society's eyes, an *ideal*, a standard that one aspires to and worships, revealing what we believe defines the 'successful entrepreneur'.

Lastly, it is important to note that not everyone believes in or subscribes to the myth. There are plenty of people (including entrepreneurs) who *criticize* entrepreneurship as it exists. In our current climate, especially, there is quite a bit of backlash against the greed or unscrupulous behaviour of certain entrepreneurs. But I think the issue runs deeper. While the financial crisis of 2008 all but ruined public faith in – and their image of – Wall Street bankers, critiques of entrepreneurs are still *reactive*. Entrepreneurs remain innocent until proven otherwise.

The myth has proven to be quite powerful culturally, because of which I believe it is imperative to understand how it shapes the beliefs of many among the general public. Why do we worship entrepreneurs? Why do we endow them with special qualities, and often privileges, that wield enormous power over the rest of society? What are we celebrating when we celebrate entrepreneurship – knowingly and unknowingly?

The myth of the entrepreneur goes something like this: the entrepreneur is born with qualities that sets him or her apart from others. The entrepreneur is *fundamentally different* from everyone else. This is why, even though entrepreneurs work with, rely on and empower others, there is some function that they alone can perform. This differential ability, most importantly, is what justifies the reward that entrepreneurs receive for their work in society.

Next, the myth proclaims that the successful entrepreneur is not only a wealth creator, but also a social value creator – by default. Entrepreneurs (automatically) create social value by providing jobs and powering the innovation that breeds social progress and economic growth. Even when entrepreneurs destroy elements of the social or economic fabric – such as when new technology upends an older industry – this 'creative destruction' is seen as necessary for the 'progress' of the system.[5]

Lastly, the myth promotes the idea that entrepreneurs are successful by merit. Many successful entrepreneurs of our time started out with very little and quickly catapulted to wealth and power. In the past, only aristocrats or the political elite had access to the kind of wealth and power now associated with entrepreneurial success. Entrepreneurship, in that sense, seems fairer, and more progressive, than previous regimes of power.

But how closely does the prevailing myth reflect our actual reality? I would like to show how, even though these three beliefs I have outlined above are often accepted unquestioningly and reinforced by institutions and cultural forces (the builders of the myth), they do not tell the full story. What the myth *leaves out*, and the implications of that, is what should be held to the light. What we are omitting through the myth is a story that is worth telling.

Before my heart attack I had rarely, if ever, questioned the myth of the entrepreneur. Instead I identified with it, living and breathing its logic. I thought the successful entrepreneur was indeed an exceptional individual who deserved massive rewards, who created social value automatically through the act of building competitive businesses, and who, for the most part, earned his success through merit.

But Vipassana reset all my deeply held beliefs. By forcing myself to reevaluate my own role in society, I was inevitably forced to interrogate entrepreneurship as a practice. What did it mean to be an entrepreneur? How did an entrepreneur create value? Where did entrepreneurs stand in our system of differential ability and rewards?

It was time to look at myself in the mirror and face the myth.

7

RULES AND REWARDS

———◆❈◆———

THE stories we tell about entrepreneurs make it seem as if their analytical ability, work ethic and/or emotional intelligence predestined them for success – a survival bias that ignores the many equally skilled individuals who did not 'fulfil their potential' due to poor timing, extenuating circumstances, or bad luck. However, popular culture often reinforces this narrative of survival bias by sensationalizing the lives of successful entrepreneurs.

To question the first assumption of the myth – that entrepreneurs possess differentiated abilities, which justifies the rewards (physical, financial, social goods/power) they get – let's first take a look at what differentiated ability is and how societies set up rules governing the rewards to those who possess it. By understanding differentiated ability and its relationship to rewards, we can look more closely at the distribution of resources in a given society. By taking a broader view of history, we can step outside our current framework and ask ourselves: do the current rules of society make sense?

Therefore, the first example I would like to begin with is an old one: human society just before the agricultural revolution, which began more than 12,000 years ago. Back then, small bands of a few dozen people roamed the world in groups referred to as hunter-gatherer communities. Even though the individuals in such communities possessed differentiated abilities with respect to hunting or scavenging, the distribution of resources in the community as a whole was strikingly egalitarian. In fact, to most hunter-gatherers, equality *despite* differentiated ability was a crucial worldview. It was part of their system of values that aided their survival as small, nomadic communities with unstable material resources.[1]

Indeed, nearly all evidence we have of hunter-gatherer societies suggests that they highly valued generosity, sharing and altruism, and they created social norms to reflect these values. For one, food sharing was central to hunter-gatherer communities – all members of one roaming band were equally entitled to food, regardless of their abilities, and social practices actively discouraged individuals from hoarding food. If a member of the community refused to share his kill, for example, Caribou Eskimos would write satirical songs making fun of the stingy person. In another example of the use of playful humour as a tool to promote and instate equality in distribution of resources, the Ju|'hoansi of southern Africa had a practice of making fun of a hunter's successful kill, calling the animal worthless or scrawny, in order to dissuade young hunters from becoming too proud or possessive and taking an outsized share or 'reward' from their kill.

And if tactics like humour did not discourage hoarders, the community would punish them, forcing them out of their fold. By constraining the overachievers from accumulating extra-personal resources and making sure the underachievers were given a portion of the shared pot, hunter-gatherers resisted the emergence of unequal distribution arising from differentiated human ability.

This did not mean that individuals with differentiated abilities in such communities were not rewarded. Highly talented individuals received respect and social prestige as the prize for their outsized contributions to the community. The best hunters were honoured with special garlands, acted in exclusive roles in religious rituals, and sat in special seats during communal gatherings. The only acceptable rewards for members with differentiated abilities were those neither fungible nor transferable: the rewards could not be exchanged or passed down to anyone else. In this way, special ability was acknowledged, yet the system of rewards and distribution maintained material and political equality within the overall community.

It may seem strange to go on this lengthy tangent about hunter-gatherers, but the point I want to make is that social norms have the power to shape the relationship between differentiated ability and distribution. It is impossible to control the natural differences among individual human beings, but human communities can set up systems and institutions that dictate how such differences are rewarded and how ability-enabled resources are distributed. Hunter-gatherer communities built egalitarian societies despite the differential abilities among them, enforcing a social code of generosity, altruism and shared resources that may seem foreign to us but was completely natural to their conception of life and survival.

Obviously, human society did not continue to maintain the strict distributive equality of the hunter-gatherer communities. Fast forward 12,000 years, and we live in a world of exponential technological advancement, globalized connectivity and unprecedented wealth creation. Somewhere along the way, we gave up the socially imposed egalitarianism of our hunter-gatherer ancestors. We moved through periods in history when resources were largely distributed based on people's birth, then to periods when resources were distributed based on people's merit. In fact, we supposedly live in an age of human history when, more so than in any other period, meritocratic rewards for differentiated ability are the norm, as opposed to the exception.

Yet when you closely examine the current distribution of wealth in the world, it is hard not to be shocked by the sheer level of inequality that stares us in the face. Although certain data points pertaining to inequality are notoriously difficult to report with accuracy, and researchers may object to the finer points of methodology in certain cited reports, it is difficult to dispute that inequality in our current world is quite extreme – and worsening. It forces us to consider whether we actually live in an era of merit, or in a continued era of birth privilege – just with a few exceptions.

All evidence seems to suggest that we are living in a world of diminishing equality – of outcomes and opportunities. Credit Suisse's 2017 Global Wealth Report showed that the top 1 per cent of the world's population now holds 50 per cent of all existing household wealth.[2] The richest forty-two individuals, a group small enough to fit into a bus, command the same amount of wealth as the poorest 3.7 billion people on Earth. Narrow that band further to the top eight billionaires in the world, and you have a group that collectively owns $450 billion in wealth. If these eight combined forces and translated their wealth into GDP, they would be the twenty-sixth largest economy in the world. The inclusion of hidden, offshore or private assets of the super-wealthy would likely reveal an even more skewed distribution of wealth.

At the other end of the spectrum, 70 per cent of the world's poorest own a meagre 3 per cent of the global wealth.[3] According to World Bank estimates, the total number of people in the world living in extreme poverty is nearly 2.5 billion. This means that a third of the world's population lives without the minimum level of income needed to secure the necessities of life.

Taking individual countries, we see that across regions wealth inequality had been rising in the period between 2007 and 2016.[4] In India, 1 per cent of the population captured 73 per cent of the new wealth created in 2017, up from 58 per cent the previous year. In the United States, the share of wealth held by the nation's richest has been steadily increasing since the 1980s, from less than 30 per cent in 1989 to 38.6 per cent in 2016, a record high since the Federal Reserve began tracking this statistic. And for the first time, the wealth share of the top 1 per cent of the population exceeded the corresponding figure for 1929, the 'Gilded Age', when many Americans believed that inequality could not get any worse.[5]

Popular pushback against the current levels of inequality has been growing for some time. From anti-establishment populist movements across the world to the popularization of Thomas Piketty's *Capital in the Twenty-First Century*, the conversation about inequality has taken centre stage.[6] To many people it appears that the problem of inequality has gotten out of hand.[7] For their 2017 report on inequality, Oxfam surveyed over 70,000 people in ten countries, and their findings suggested high levels of discontent about inequality: more than 75 per cent of those surveyed either agreed or strongly agreed that the gap between the rich and the poor in their country was too large, and the same majority preferred lower levels of income inequality than what existed in their country. In fact, more than half the people surveyed expressed the desire for lower levels of inequality in their country than currently existed in any country. Period.

———

Yet, just because there is something offensive about inequality does not mean that there is something fundamentally wrong with it. After all, for most of human history inequality of wealth and power has been even more extreme. In the age of empires, it was not uncommon for the few individuals with close relations to rulers to enrich themselves enormously while most of the subjects lived in abject poverty. Class differences were more rigid in those times and wealth almost always came from corrupt sources. In the feudal ages, a few landlords owned most of the wealth, feasted on meat and fine wine and hosted lavish gatherings in their castles while the vast majority of the general populace led lives of forced labour barely above subsistence level.

Considering all this, is it really so wrong to reward those who, through their own hard work and ingenuity, achieved success in modern business? Is inequality, even in the era of democratization and increased social mobility, simply a necessary byproduct of economic growth?

In order to condemn inequality, our reference point must go beyond the question of taste; we have to establish that there is something tangibly bad about inequality. Thankfully, many scholars have dedicated their time to much reputed research, cataloguing how high levels of inequality (in both income and wealth) negatively impact society as a whole. So, there are real reasons for concern about inequality, as various negative phenomena correlate to or are affected by it.[8]

For one, people living in countries with higher economic inequality tend to live shorter, more stressful and far less healthy lives. Inequality is linked to health problems such as obesity, mental illness, drug abuse and teenage births.[9] These problems are primarily found among the poorer classes, but the wealthy are affected too, since inequality decreases social cohesion, making life more stressful and less secure for all.

Less social cohesion, a hallmark of unequal societies, means that people in a society are less likely to trust each other, less likely to feel they belong, less likely to engage in social or civic action, and more likely to act in competitive and insecure ways because of 'status anxiety'.[10] Both property crime and crimes of violence (homicide, murder and robbery) have been shown to be strongly related to worsening income inequality.[11]

There is an argument that inequality of outcome (such as income or wealth) is not important at all, as long as we have equality of *opportunity*.[12] However, economic inequality actually *erodes* the social mobility that allows for equality of opportunity. According to a 2012 study by political scientist Miles Corak, countries with high income inequality such as Peru, Brazil and Argentina have higher levels of intergenerational earning elasticity – that is, the earnings of one generation have a higher impact on the earnings of the next – than do countries with lower income inequality, likely because highly unequal societies allow the wealthier classes to retreat to isolated institutions and opportunities meant for them alone.[13] This means that in unequal societies, not only are individuals less able to live a better life than their parents' generation, but they are also more likely to be stuck in the same bad economic situation all their lives. In this way, inequality of outcome *contributes* to inequality of opportunity.[14]

Lastly, economists have shown that inequality on the scale that modern entrepreneurs have sustained and allowed with their disproportionate payoffs can stunt overall economic growth. There are many reasons why inequality is destructive to growth, including the fact that nations with high inequality often have large lower-income populations with no access to healthcare or education, and have no system in place to turn those citizens into productive, socially mobile and growth-contributing members of society. Also, economies that are deeply unequal also report higher levels of inflation, instability and institutional and personal debt. Higher economic inequality has also been linked to a higher frequency of financial crises, whereas one sees more sustained growth in more equal societies.[15]

To be fair, there is no consensus as to how inequality affects growth. In fact, certain economists and politicians adamantly oppose the idea that inequality negatively affects growth, and there is mixed evidence for inequality and growth when the rates are compared for different countries. However, I believe that a more general analogy is more appropriate here. It is not that any incremental increase in inequality necessarily means a proportionate decrease in economic growth. But, as a rule, when societies become increasingly unequal, the *incentives* for social groups change in a way that could choke off growth.[16]

The most symbolic example of inequality choking off growth and innovation is perhaps the story of medieval Venice, one of the most innovative, competitive and open economies of its time. As inequality slowly grew in Venice, with profits accumulating in the hands of a small class of merchants, the new-generation elite decided that holding onto their own interest was more important than addressing the concerns of the general economy. The elite changed Venice's trading laws. A small group of families ended up hoarding most of the city's wealth. Venice changed from an open economy to a closed one, from a potential democracy to an oligarchy.

Within a decade, the prosperity of the city-kingdom plunged. The city stopped growing even as other European cities began to flourish. Venetians called this era La Serrata, or 'The Closing', which should be a reminder to us that the misaligned incentives for the elite can mean consolidation of power in the short term but ultimately self-destruction in the long term.

I suspect we are living in a similar age, when the misaligned incentives for those who profit from highly unequal systems is eroding the possibility of an inclusive and innovative world economy. This is why the capitalist system which promotes entrepreneurship has a self-destructive core: the system promotes developments that destroy the very conditions that made its existence possible.

———

When I began thinking and obsessing over these questions of inequality and the purpose of entrepreneurship, I had countless conversations with my friends and fellow entrepreneurs. In public, many of these individuals criticized inequality or boasted about their philanthropic activity as evidence that they wanted to be part of the solution. Some of them, especially ultra-rich entrepreneurs from societies with already unstable social relations, often downplayed their personal wealth to the general audience.

But my conversations about inequality took place in the private enclaves of the wealthy: over tasting menus at Michelin-starred restaurants; inside clubhouses scattered across London, New York, Tokyo; over drinks at networking sessions or business conferences. This was a tight-knit global community that mostly kept to their own, isolating themselves into a highly exclusive set of well-endowed, well-connected individuals.

When I posed my questions to my peers as to what they felt about their wealth in the face of the stark global inequality in existence, the responses ranged from evasive to shocking. Some tried to be politically correct without making any real commitments. 'Inequality is certainly bad,' they would say, 'But as entrepreneurs, we are already doing what we can by creating jobs. Besides, there is no real alternative.'

Some others offered the cynical argument that the current system reflected an unchangeable fact of human nature. 'The world is made up of winners and losers, Ravi,' one entrepreneur in Hong Kong said, patting my back. 'Introduce me to one poor person who would bat an eye before trading places with a winner. They wouldn't care about your suffering then, trust me.' Many simply believed that my claim – that a more equal distribution was not only just, but good for social progress – was wrong altogether.

To those who were more receptive, I posed a simple question that pushed against the prevailing myth that the rules and rewards system in our society was fair. What actually generates wealth in an economy, and who benefits from it? If we try to understand how rewards are allocated in society, we soon discover that the already wealthy are the main beneficiaries of our growing economy – and by a long shot. In fact, a stupefying 82 per cent of all growth in global wealth in 2017 accrued to the top 1 per cent, while the bottom 50 per cent of humanity experienced no increase in wealth whatsoever. Since the financial crisis in 2008, most of the new wealth in the world has gone to the top wealth holders.

One major reason for this is that in our world, the financial returns from capital (assets like stocks and real estate) far outpace the earnings from wage employment. Between 2006 and 2015, billionaire wealth grew by almost 13 per cent every year, most of which was generated by returns to capital, e.g., interest payments, rising share prices or property appreciation. Contrast this with the earnings of the vast majority of the world's population that *only* generates wealth through wages, which grew just 2 per cent per year on average over the same period. The return to capital outpaced the return to labour by almost six times.

The problem with such disproportionately high returns on capital over earnings from wages is that capital is highly concentrated amongst the wealthy. Most people do not have the initial wealth or access to generate rewards from capital. In fact, the uneven distribution of financial capital, such as stocks, mirrors the uneven distribution of wealth around the world: globally, the top 1 per cent of wealthiest individuals own about 55 per cent of all such assets.

In addition to this, even among those who only generate wealth in the form of wages or salary, rewards to top earners grew significantly more than rewards to low- or middle-skilled labour, further worsening wealth inequality. According to research by the Economic Policy Institute, between 1978 and 2013, CEO compensation in the US increased 937 per cent, nearly 90 times as much as the 10.2 per cent growth of the median worker's compensation.[17] Similar trends exist across the world: median wages decline, while top earners see skyrocketing pay-cheques. This lands us right back into another situation of uneven gains between capital and labour.

These figures shook me to the very bone. They drew a picture of a winner-takes-all economy where the most advantaged positions within the system received the most substantial rewards.

How do entrepreneurs fit into this system of differentiated ability and rewards? I believe that entrepreneurs play two roles in this story: one as beneficiaries, and the other as architects.

As an entrepreneur myself, I believe in the necessity of *some* reward for entrepreneurs, all of whom take on significant risk to build profitable ventures. If everyone were guaranteed to receive the same amount of resources at all times, then what would encourage entrepreneurs to take on the risks they do?

Yet, today, the differentiated ability of a few entrepreneurs brings them gigantic, unfathomably high rewards. Indeed, entrepreneurs are some of the greatest beneficiaries of the rules-and-rewards system in the economy currently. It is no coincidence that seven out of eight of the wealthiest billionaires in the world are entrepreneurs. Out of the eight, only one started out with any inheritance or family legacy. Becoming an entrepreneur and generating wealth from one's own company is the ultimate golden ticket: if successful, an entrepreneur can, within his or her lifetime, generate the same amount of wealth as millions of working people would in their entire lives.

The absolute increase in creation of wealth means that the wealthiest entrepreneurs today are massively wealthier than the wealthiest among their previous generations. For example, Bill Gates's fortune, amounting to $75.4 billion in February 2016, was roughly 1 million times as much as the average US household income. Daniel Ludwig, a comparable entrepreneur in the 1980s, had a fortune of 'just' 50,000 times the average household income.

The more insidious aspect of extreme wealth, beyond its ability to purchase or consume goods, is that this wealth easily translates into political and cultural power. Such wealth influences elections, shapes (or in some cases, controls) media, lobbies for its own benefit, dictates cultural trends and influences our lives in ways that most people will never know about. The Eskimo would be confused by this inversion: in our world, personal accumulation of material resources translates into political and cultural power. In the Eskimo's world, only giving away and sharing material resources could have such an effect.

When I asked myself why the world worked this way, I could not come up with any satisfactory answers. Although I was not someone who would advocate forced equality of outcomes for every member of society, what made me very uncomfortable was the sheer *scale* of the difference in rewards, and how easily entrepreneurs like myself could translate disproportionate wealth into political and cultural power. Warren Buffett summed up this idea of disproportionate rewards quite well in his Giving Pledge letter, explaining his decision to give away 99 per cent of his assets to charity:

> I've worked in an economy that rewards someone who saves the lives of others on a battlefield with a medal, rewards a great teacher with thank-you notes from parents, but rewards those who can detect the mispricing of securities with sums reaching into the billions. In short, fate's distribution of long straws is wildly capricious.

What if entrepreneurs were not allowed billion-dollar rewards? What if they received smaller payoffs, or perhaps even non-financial payoffs, for their differentiated ability, as in the Eskimo model? Who is to say, in that situation, that all entrepreneurs would not suddenly decide that their life's work was not worth doing? In fact, the entrepreneurs I respected most were all people who saw financial gain as only a secondary effect of building businesses. Indeed, many took on the uncertainty and struggles of building their own enterprises while making less financial gains than they might have in high-profile corporate positions. Some of them worked on socially-minded projects, while others were just enthusiasts of a particular industry or technology.

The chief motivation, in these cases, was the actual building of the business itself, the fulfilment of some personal goal or passion. The incentive was the process, not the reward. Yet we do not broadcast *these* entrepreneurial stories. Indeed, the danger of the myth of the entrepreneur is that it places power and visibility primarily in the hands of the wealth-creating entrepreneur, founders with mind-boggling net worths. They remain the ones uniquely positioned to shape our culture.

Entrepreneurs also play a unique role as *architects* of reward systems. Since it is the entrepreneurs who set the 'DNA' of their own ventures, they have the power to decide how the wealth and opportunities created by their business are distributed, and the kind of culture and values embedded in the business itself.

Although they cannot control every aspect of their business, entrepreneurs certainly can set the tone or a precedent within their ventures, some of which could have a significant positive impact on unequal rewards. For instance, to what extent does the company share profits with employees, in the form of stock options or other mechanisms? Who are the company's investors, and how aggressively do they demand payouts? What is the acceptable ratio between executive pay (including stocks) and the average worker's pay? Does the company do business with other entities that violate fair and safe labour standards or do not pay a living wage?

Many entrepreneurs, myself included, still fail to act on these matters. Part of this is due to complacency. As individuals, we become comfortable in our insulated social groups made up of people just like ourselves, and we gradually come to believe that our own disproportionate rewards are natural. We begin comparing how much *less* we have than the wealthier, more successful peers around us, not how much more we have than almost all other people on Earth.

At the same time, we are also focused on the success of the business, which is measured by the profits it brings its shareholders rather than by other forms of value it may create. What if generous employee packages mean that investors look elsewhere for higher returns? What if refusing to pay a CEO hundreds of times as much as his employees means that we cannot recruit the best talent? In short, what if social concerns render our for-profit businesses less competitive, and thus doom them to failure, especially if most of the other businesses out there operate on profit-first rules? The most that entrepreneurs can do, it seems, is to wait until retirement to redirect some of their good fortunes to philanthropy.

What worries me is that this type of complacent, passive social engagement on the part of entrepreneurs will create even more trouble in the future, since all indications suggest that existing tensions and trends are only going to make inequality worse, not better. In fact, without any social reorganization or corrective mechanisms in place, inequality (and all its negative effects) may get much, much worse in the coming decades, to the point of pushing our current social systems to breaking point.

There are various parallel changes happening to our society that may further ignite the slow, steady flame of growing inequality. For example, labour automation. Since Adam Smith theorized about capitalism in 1776, automation has been seen in economic theory as an inevitable process. Though automation may initially result in the displacement of workers, many economists believe it will eventually rebalance the system at an equilibrium of higher productivity.[18]

The story goes like this. Automation allows one person to do the work of many – or in the case of autonomous robots, one machine to do the work of many – resulting in an increase in productivity. The entrepreneur, who is now able to produce more goods at the same cost, is able to lower prices and beat out competitors, thus increasing profits. Supposedly, this surplus profit enables the entrepreneur to invest that money back into the business and pay higher wages to the remaining employees. Over time, the jobs that were initially taken away from workers return in different forms or fields. Wages increase overall, and the efficiency of the production processes passes on to consumers through lower prices of goods.[19]

In the nineteenth and twentieth centuries, the automation of agriculture into an industrial business led to unemployed farmers flooding into urban centres looking for jobs in manufacturing. In the mid-twentieth century, automation, in the form of automated switchboards and control systems, replaced employees in traditional manufacturing, so workers migrated to the service industry. In the twenty-first century, computerization began automating those service jobs too, creating space for what we call the 'sharing' or 'gig economy' of contractual workers and peer-to-peer services.

The difference between these various historical periods of automation lies in the answer to the question: whom do the extra wealth and productivity created by automation benefit?

Until recently, increasing productivity did mean an increase in profit for entrepreneurs, but it also meant an increase in wages for workers, since workers were freed from menial tasks and trained for higher-skill jobs. The story more or less correlated with Adam Smith's version of events.

Yet, as Martin Ford writes in *Rise of the Machines*, '... that symbiotic increasing productivity and rising wages began to dissolve in the 1970s.'[20] In 2013, a typical American manufacturing worker earned 13 per cent *less* than the real value he or she would have earned in 1973, even though productivity rose 107 per cent in the same period. As we enter this new era of automation, the wealth that accrues from increasing productivity is overwhelmingly enriching the owners or shareholders of businesses, but not workers. The most enriched shareholders are often the founding entrepreneurs themselves, or wealthy individuals who hold far more stocks in these companies than other segments of society do. All in all, it seems that Adam Smith's vision of a shared prosperity from productivity growth is suffering a breakdown.

The outlook for workers is even more bleak. In the past, automation could only target repetitive physical functions. Now we have robots that can perform a variety of non-routine and specialized tasks, such as operation of an entire assembly line (Tesla), restocking of shelves in warehouses (Amazon), and 3-D printing of sneakers (Adidas's Speedfactory). Companies like Rethink Robots are training robots to complete tasks outside the conveyor belt; in 2012, they built a three-foot-tall robot named Baxter which can learn new skills through training and upload its 'knowledge' to other robots through a USB device.

We are entering an age where automation can replace human repetitive cognitive functions too, not just physical labour. With the development of artificial intelligence, machines that mimic human cognitive functions like learning and problem-solving will become commonplace.[21] Pizza Hut outlets in Japan have already piloted a humanoid robot that can take orders, process payments and analyse your facial expressions to recommend other products using AI technology. Traditional white-collar jobs, like insurance, bookkeeping, managing investment portfolios, legal research and basic human resources are now vulnerable to automation. A 2013 paper by a group of Oxford academics titled 'The Future of Employment' concludes that within two decades, almost 50 per cent of all jobs in the US will be vulnerable to automation.[22]

Entrepreneurs welcome labour-displacing (automating) technologies because it increases productivity while decreasing costs. Robots and smart machines are, in essence, the perfect workers. They act in uniformity and with precision. They rarely make mistakes. They do not need to eat, drink water, sleep or take coffee breaks. They do not demand benefits like vacations or healthcare and are highly unlikely to organize and revolt against their bosses.

This tendency to automate at any human cost is summed up simply by Nike's solution to the problem of rising wages in Indonesian factories (which is around $0.50 an hour): 'engineer the labor out of the product.' Do not rely on humans. This is the most cost-effective and profit-maximizing solution of all.

———

All this may seem quite pessimistic, and I fear that I am going to be unpopular for writing this book. Entrepreneurs are supposed to be the optimists in the automation discussion, championing labour-displacing innovation as a way of creating new industries that humans have not yet explored. Automation does not replace jobs, many of my peers argue, they *displace* jobs for a period, then allow people to work on more higher-level, interesting things. Surely this is a win-win situation.

If you meet anyone who knows me, they will attest to my having always been a technology geek. Since I was young, I have always been intrigued by cutting-edge technology, whether it was telecommunications in the 1990s or renewable energy today. I am not deriding technological development because I am someone who is scared of, or turned off by, technology itself.

The liberating potential of technology is enormous. If wielded in the correct environment and context, AI and automation could produce a society of abundance. A large variety of high-quality goods could be produced more efficiently than ever before in human history. Ultimately, human beings could be freed from all boring, repetitive tasks, and could instead focus their time on creative, life-affirming projects. Advances in genetic technology could mean the elimination of hereditary illnesses and improved quality of life for many.

But nothing happens in a vacuum, and the environment in which this unprecedented technological automation is happening suggests a less rosy picture. A 2017 Mckinsey report on the state of automation says that 30 per cent to 45 per cent of the working-age population around the world is already effectively underutilized – meaning they are either unemployed, inactive or underemployed.[23] The rise of contractual work in the developed countries means that many workers do not receive the benefits usually reserved for full-time employees. Around the world, wages are stagnant or are failing to increase as fast as the cost of education and healthcare. Middle-class jobs are disappearing into a polarized labour market, with highly-skilled, educated workers at one end and low-skilled and extremely low-paid workers at the other.

It is hard for a technology-enabled utopia to bloom in our present system of rewards and protection. Only the wealthy have access to the abundance of technology, while the rest are left behind. We must face the reality that our global economy is no longer a win-win situation, but a winner-takes-all situation. The entrepreneurs and shareholders at the top of the pyramid reap the rewards from productivity gains while everyone else may be left by the wayside. The result is a world divided into two: the plutocrats (who enjoy the plenitude and abundance of technology), and the rest.

It is up to those who benefit from the system to better shape it for the needs of the future.

8

THE GOOD, THE BAD AND
THE UGLY

❖

A S I HAVE repeatedly stated, the myth of the entrepreneur is not false or intentionally deceiving, but it is an incomplete story. Entrepreneurs *do* possess a special, differentiated ability, and the successful ones translate this ability into functioning, profitable businesses. But differentiated ability does not mean that our current distribution of resources is fair. In fact, the scale of extreme wealth that has been distributed to individual entrepreneurs as a reward for their differentiated ability is, in my opinion, self-destructive.

You can imagine that none of this has made me a particularly pleasant or popular dinner companion among my peers. Over the past few years I've been invited to fewer and fewer social affairs. Even Helen sometimes asks me why I am so intent on this subject. It is not an uplifting topic, so to speak, and I am not a very diplomatic spokesperson.

Looking back, I admit that I have not always expressed my beliefs in the best way. What I should have done, rather than make my friends feel that they were being shamed by the state of inequality, was to express a kind of *optimistic urgency*.

By the end of the current century, technological advancement, climate change and a changing balance of power in the world have the potential to reshape life on Earth as we know it. In the face of this, *optimism*, a crucial ingredient, reminds us that seizing this moment with principled agency could make all the difference.

We, as entrepreneurs, could choose to expand our horizons, redefine value creation through a collectivist and compassionate mindset, and put serious thought into how our current system of rules and rewards could evolve. We could be actively working with others (academics, activists, artists) to build a better, more equitable future, or we could sit back as the few who are fortunate enough to have an escape plan if things do not turn out well.

I did not have much confidence in my capacity for optimistic persuasion when these thoughts first started brewing in my head, so instead of refining my message, I turned inwards. My one burning thought was, how could I create an entrepreneurial venture where the rewards did *not* go to myself, but created value for a collective beyond the individual? How could I practise my differentiated ability – the ability to build businesses using clever models and tangential solutions – while upholding a new understanding of value creation?

In my view, there were two important elements to this. The first was to structure a business where the majority of financial profits did not end up in the hands of a few. The financial value should not be directed to make disproportionate gain for myself or other wealthy investors, but distributed to the neediest in society. The second was to structure a business that empowered individuals and groups within the organization and promoted their holistic well-being.

I have seen, through the years, people around me walking away from a life centred on personal gain. Some of them then pursued different, socially-oriented occupations in non-profit sectors. Others turned to teaching, public service or philanthropy. But I did not want to leave entrepreneurship altogether. I wanted the best of both worlds – I wanted to still engage in the activity I loved while eliminating what I saw as its destructive contradiction. I wanted to see if I could perhaps reconcile the tension between my passion and my responsibility to society. This reconciliation would always be a work in progress or, to go back to Vipassana, something that invoked that feeling of cognitive dissonance. It would be imperfect and evolving, and I had to question my progress every step of the way. But I had to try.

———

If my aim was to build a competitive, profitable business where the rewards were not concentrated in the hands of a few, then I needed to design a company starting with some unique first principles. The opportunistic thinking that defined the tangential solution, the core philosophy of my earlier businesses, would not be enough.

The first principle I set was *longevity*. To channel maximal resources back into society, I needed to build a business that could survive generations, as opposed to the five-to-ten-year lifespans of my previous businesses.

The second was *scale*. I wanted to push my own personal boundaries of $100 million businesses and aim for a company that could be an order of magnitude larger; this would ensure the largest amount of capital for redistribution. I gave myself an ambitious target – to build a $10 billion company in ten years' time.

Now all I had to do was to come up with a business idea.

One morning I was riding on the London Tube after my walk around South Park, a beautiful clearing near my home. I have always loved the experience of riding the Tube – something about the blue cushioned seats and the people reading newspapers on their way to work charmed me with its careful and efficient rhythm. This city has charisma, I thought to myself. My gaze turned to the older gentleman sitting across from me, who was intensely scanning every page of the *Guardian* laid across his lap.

I looked out of the window and my mind invariably wandered to my homeland, and I thought about how Mumbai, a city infamous for its congestion, could benefit from such a metro system. In fact, one was in the process of being built. A few stations had opened in the city, and the rest were to be completed by 2021. I felt a familiar tinge of sadness to think about the poor state of Indian infrastructure, and how much investment and effort was needed to even come close to bringing more efficient and technologically advanced public transportation to the public.

This line of thought, as I was riding on the London tube, led me to seriously consider whether there was a possible business opportunity in that space. I had never considered an infrastructure business before, for many reasons. Most glaringly, the industry has a bad reputation for corruption and cronyism in its close dealings with the government.

I also recognized that India's infrastructure sector is markedly different from that of other countries. In most economies, most of the public infrastructure is built and owned by the government, from the US highway system to China's high-speed rail network. Yet starting in 2004, either by design or deliberate abdication, India started allowing private ownership of major public infrastructure. It was the only large economy in the world where assets such as major airports, thousands of kilometres of road, national ports and utilities, were being built completely by the private sector. With a country of India's population and size, the growing privatization of its infrastructure sector could be the largest creator of private wealth in the world, on the scale of trillions of dollars over the next decade.

Infrastructure fit both my objectives: longevity and scale. Infrastructure assets are long-term, lasting anywhere from ten to 100 years. Infrastructure presented opportunities for scale, projected to constitute a $5 trillion market in India over the next twenty years, which would be one of the largest instances of wealth creation in the country. My goal of building a $10 billion company would only be a small piece of a huge pie.

So, I started to examine this industry. The one barrier was that infrastructure is *very* capital-intensive; it required huge amounts of money, both equity and debt. My usual tactic had been to retain majority ownership of my companies through creative financing without putting down much money of my own, but in this case, creative financing would not be enough to tackle the sheer amount of capital that these businesses required.

This was the first major hurdle I faced. For instance, I considered entering the airport business, but I was late to the game. Most of the major airports (Mumbai, Delhi, Bengaluru) were already auctioned off on thirty-year contracts, and the successful bidders who won those contracts were companies that already had their own billion-dollar balance sheets. Roads and ports were a similar story – established players were putting up billions of dollars to participate in their building and running.

The sector that interested me due to its growth potential was power and utilities. When I was just beginning to draw up these ideas in 2009, India was generating around 200 gigawatts of power per annum. Yet, to reach power to the 400 million without access to power or electricity, India needed to add over 1,500 gigawatts of generating capacity. This meant that the power industry alone required about $1.5 trillion's worth of investments. Yet the dominant power sources (coal and fossil fuel) were businesses that also required starting capital to the tune of $1 billion.

My initial findings evoked a strong sense of déjà vu: it was like trying to enter the telecommunications industry all over again, a relative nobody trying to break into an industry of giants. Some things had not changed after all these years. I still did not want to put up money of my own, nor did I want to give away majority ownership of the company to a bank or investor who would foot the billion-dollar bill with their investment.

Slightly frustrated by the dead ends I fetched up, I was relieved when my good friend Audun called me to suggest that I visit him in Iceland. He was the first person I had met while at Stanford Business School – a quirky, warm man with a proverbial heart of gold. It would clear my head, I thought, to get away from London for a while.

In Iceland, Audun and I spent five days hiking, from Landmannalaugar, a natural reserve in southern Iceland, to Holaskjol. The landscape of glaciers looked extraterrestrial, with sepia- and blue-toned mountains hovering in the background of massive sheets of ice. There was nobody in sight for miles and no specific path, but we went by a general route Audun's friend had suggested. We set out with forty-pound backpacks stuffed with food, a tent, GPS devices, two sleeping bags, plenty of optimism, and a few beers.

The landscape was unlike any I had tackled before. First, we needed to cross a glacial river, a body of water so piercingly blue it was as if someone had poured thousands of gallons of mouthwash between the ice sheets. Adding to the difficulty was the constantly meandering path of the glacial river; there was no way to tell how many times we would need to cross it before reaching our destination. We ended up crossing the river eleven times, holding hands and wading through water that was so freezing cold you could see tiny icebergs floating on its surface.

After five days, Audun and I reached a vividly green plain at the edge of the glacier. On that plain I could see a semi-circular pool in the ground, bubbling with steaming water.

'What in the world is *that*?' I asked Audun.

'It's a geothermal pool,' he said matter-of-factly. 'It's also our treat at the end of the hike.' And with that, he unzipped his snowsuit, ran towards the pool of water and jumped in, feet first. My jaw dropped.

'Come on, Ravi!' Audun laughed when he saw the bewildered expression on my face. 'You haven't had a shower in five days either.'

I gave him a look of warning, muttered under my breath, and jumped in. The water had a strong smell of sulphur, but its steamy heat felt like heaven after days of hiking in the frigid Icelandic air.

'This is amazing,' I said with a long sigh. 'Nature's hot tub.' We both leaned back to rest our arms on the edge of the pool and let the bubbling water massage our weary muscles.

'It is a beautiful feat of nature, indeed,' Audun replied. 'When I was a kid, my dad would come back from work smelling like this. Whenever I sit in a pool, I think of him.'

'Really? What did he do?'

'He was an engineer designing geothermal energy plants.'

This piqued my interest. 'A geothermal energy plant? So how does that work?'

'With beautiful simplicity, if you ask me. Just 400-degree Fahrenheit water and steam coming up from below the earth at very high pressure. This high-pressure water runs the turbines of the plant, and is then pumped back down into the ground. It's a very efficient process. At my Dad's plant, only two engineers needed to oversee the whole thing.'

What a cool operation, I thought. High efficiency, operationally lean, and completely renewable. Could this be the answer I was looking for?

———

When I touched down at Heathrow airport, my mind felt clear. I was happy that I was able to reconnect with one of my best friends, but the cherry on the cake was that I now had a whole new business direction to investigate: renewable energy.

I did not previously consider renewable energy because I thought it was not an economically viable industry. On the surface, renewables appeared to be an industry propped up by subsidies, the government's version of financial aid for industries they want to support for reasons beyond profitability. It was my belief that an industry dependent on government subsidies always had to prioritize management of political risk, something incredibly difficult and which, in many cases, meant dealing with corruption.

In Iceland, however, I witnessed renewable, geothermal power that was profitable without any government assistance. Renewable energy was simply one competitive sector of the overall power market. Audun was even kind enough to give me a personal tour of a geothermal plant run by Reykjavik Energy near his home, and I saw the 'beautiful simplicity' he spoke of in action.

In India, too, renewable energy was becoming economically viable. Technological innovation and diminishing costs meant that the economics and the engineering finally made sense. Wind turbine vendors like Vestas and Suzlon were already operating wind farms, which produced nearly 10 gigawatts of power. What I found even more surprising was that these projects were price-competitive with traditional energy sources such as coal.

However, even though renewable energy in India seemed to be reaching a turning point in terms of economic viability, it remained underdeveloped in its ownership structure. Although India did not have a tariff subsidy for renewables, the government still actively tried to use its power to grow the industry by running an accelerated depreciation scheme for renewables assets. What that fancy term means is that the government gave owners of renewables assets (e.g., wind farms or solar panels) a multi-year tax deferral.

Therefore, in India, an industry of passive owners developed and hardened into the status quo: wind farms were owned mostly by big companies and rich individuals, including quite a few celebrities, who 'owned' one or two megawatts of wind or solar power on their balance sheets so they could receive an annual tax write-off. The only active participants in the sector were the turbine vendors, who built, managed and operated the wind farms in the name of these passive owners.

Despite this scenario, the more I delved into my research, the more excited I became about renewable energy. The Indian government pledged to support at least 300 gigawatts of renewable energy by 2030, ten times the country's current capacity, making renewables a guaranteed growth industry of significant size. Globally, renewables are a future-facing industry, something that will likely become a significant part of the world's energy makeup, as costs decrease and demand for non-polluting energy sources increases.

The deciding factor was my realization that a renewable energy business could be creatively financed: since windmills take about one year to build, as opposed to the five-to-ten-year build-time for other infrastructure assets, a renewable energy company could technically be funded, at least in part, by internal cash flows. This just meant that it was possible to take the money you made within the business annually and invest in more projects, which lowered the capital requirements to get started.

Renewables hit all the points I needed. It was of the right scale, it had long-term potential, and it was the right marketplace. But I had no experience in the industry, no assets, no desire to put down any money of my own, and had a firm intent to retain majority ownership of the company. I knew that this would seem preposterous to almost anyone I approached, especially investors.

I always believed that part of being an entrepreneur lies in learning how to be a small guy who dresses up in a big man's clothes. You need to tell a story with so much conviction that people believe in your vision, even if you don't have the deepest pockets. Luckily, this is also my greatest strength: to create compelling narratives from ideas that convince people much brighter and more powerful than me to take a stake in my projects.

The first thing I did to set up a renewables business was to acquire a brand. This was a very strange step for an entrepreneur, almost unheard of. But after some very persistent following up, I finally landed a meeting with Lord Swraj Paul, a businessman and founder of the Caparo Group, a steel and auto-components conglomerate based in London. People around the world knew the Caparo name, so associating with them provided instant credibility.

I approached Lord Swraj Paul with a most unusual request, namely, that he license the Caparo brand to my company that was yet to be formed. The licence, which would last ten years, meant simply that I could use the Caparo name for my companies and subsidiaries. In exchange, Lord Paul would receive a share of the renewables energy business I intended to build.

It was not an easy story to sell, but I eventually convinced Lord Paul that his association with the renewable-energy business would be positive. Not only would his share in the company grow, but this was an opportunity to get an inside look into an industry in India with unprecedented growth prospects.

I still remember sitting in his grand office on Baker Street in London, my gaze meeting his; I with only an idea in my head and this stately man with an industrial empire of his own, whose desk was littered with awards and letters from the House of Lords. Lord Paul was a discerning and shrewd businessman, but even more than that, he was an Indian who had made himself into a powerful figure at the heart of English society.

He looked me up and down, at the entrepreneur who had spent the past five years wandering around and reflecting on the meaning of life. Even though he could not understand this gap in my curriculum vitae, he could sense the optimistic urgency in me which suggested that even if this did not work out, I would find other ways of building what I needed to build. Such is the power of creating something for purposes beyond one's personal gain.

'Why should I do this for you?' he asked me one last time at the end of our hour-long meeting.

I decided to be as honest and straightforward as possible. 'I am a man of my word.' I said, looking directly into his eyes. 'And if I succeed, you will be a businessman linked to one of the most exciting industries in India today.'

In two weeks we settled on an agreement. The brand licence was mine.

———

That summer, serendipity, an unpalpable yet all-powerful force of life, struck in the form of my nephew Vikram, who showed up on my doorstep in Hyderabad. I will never forget that moment when I saw him, walking up to my door briskly and confidently with a beaming smile on his face. Even in the most stressful and pressured circumstances, Vikram can light up an entire room with his genuine optimism; he is a natural leader. I waved for him to come inside at once.

'When did you come to Hyderabad?' I asked, when we sat down. The past few years, I had visited Vikram whenever I was in New York, where he was working as an investment banker at Credit Suisse. Often it would be only late on Sunday afternoons that his boss would release him, and the two of us would hurry to a midtown bar to properly catch up for an hour or two. We had talked about his desire to move back to India, but I did not know that he was already back in the country.

'Just two days ago,' Vikram said. 'You are one of the first people I am seeing.'

'Welcome home.' I gave him one of my rare hugs.

Ever since he was young, Vikram and I had shared a special relationship. His father had passed away when he was twelve, and Vikram's mother – a woman of incredible perseverance and faith – raised her two sons alone. They grew up in a one-room home in Hyderabad, a family of three and a loyal German Shepherd.

Even though we were distant relatives in a large, extended family, I took a liking to Vikram. When he was a child, he would always pass by my house on the weekends. He was a precocious and hyperactive boy who was always chattering away, brimming with questions and observations. His mother would often bemoan the most recent instance of Vikram's mischief, but always with a smile playing on her lips. His energy required some taming, but that same energy also made him the joy of so many people's lives.

Beneath his restless energy, Vikram also possessed a formidable intelligence, both academically and practically. I watched him progress from secondary school in Hyderabad to IIT Madras, one of the most prestigious engineering institutes in India, and then to Yale Business School. After finishing his studies, he embarked on a successful career in finance. At each stage of his progress, I offered what little advice or help I could. And now he was here, back in Hyderabad.

'So, Vikram, tell me. What is the next step for you?'

'I'd like to be an entrepreneur, Uncle, and start my own business here in India.'

I was not surprised; ever since he was young, Vikram has been the enterprising sort. 'Do you have any idea what you'd like to do?'

'Not yet. My best friend from IIT has decided to work with me, so at least I have a partner. We will spend the next few months brainstorming and crafting a business plan.'

I reminded him that I was there for him and would be happy to give advice, introduce him to people in my network and act a sounding board; essentially, to make sure his transition was as smooth as possible.

Although I did not mention it at the time, I had the budding thought that perhaps Vikram would like to work together on the renewables company I was building. Even though he was only twenty-six, he was undoubtedly bright, and someone I could trust professionally and personally. By sheer coincidence, Vikram had renewables experience since he was placed in an alternative energy group at Credit Suisse, where he had worked on some major financing deals in the industry. He undoubtedly understood more about renewable energy than I did.

I silenced these thoughts for one reason: I had a policy about never working with family, for both moral and historical reasons. Although it was the norm in India to establish family businesses and include family members in entrepreneurial ventures, I found such nepotism or favouritism to be unproductive and toxic. It was better, I believed, to build meritocratic organizations that judged people on ability alone, and not by their proximity or relationship to the founder. The historical record in our family bore out the same evidence: partnerships between Kailas family members had resulted in hurt feelings, lost assets or, more often than not, both. I valued my relationship with Vikram too much to risk that. Plus, he had come back to India to carry out *his* dream. Perhaps working with me would stifle that.

Eventually, it was Vikram who broke the silence, a month after his arrival. We were sitting in my balcony in Hyderabad, overlooking the leafy forest and white stucco facades of Jubilee Hills. It was just before sunset, and the sky was glowing a deep tangerine pink.

'Uncle, if you do not agree, you can forget I ever mentioned it.' I was surprised by the nervousness in Vikram's voice and turned my attention to him.

'What is it?' I asked.

'We've already spent so many evenings talking about the renewables business. I think it's an incredible opportunity, and an area where I happen to have some experience. But we never talk about working *together*.' Vikram then listed all the reasons why a partnership would be a good idea – his banking experience in renewables, our implicit trust in each other, and his insatiable desire to learn about doing business in India.

I had already thought about these points, and was happy to hear him repeat my sentiments. In fact, over the course of a few months, my initial reservations about working with Vikram diminished day by day. Not only did I think we could structure a professional relationship that did not jeopardize our personal one, but I also realized that working with Vikram would bring real value to the business.

The next time we met, Vikram and I sat down and wrote what we now call 'The Ten Commandments', a document outlining the expectations and basic principles of our partnership. We stipulated Vikram's role, the timeline of his commitment, and my promise to give him as much exposure as possible. In fact, that was the one thing Vikram stressed – he wanted to be involved in all parts of the business in order to learn as much as possible about being an entrepreneur in India. I was moved by his dedication, and added the following clause at the bottom of our agreement:

Ravi will do everything possible to ensure that Vikram gets the best learning from this experience (i.e., provide opportunities, give responsibility, share everything about the business *the good, the bad, the ugly*'). Essentially treat Vikram as his other self.

We did not know what kind of a team we would make. Only time would tell.

———

With step one of my plan (acquiring a brand) complete, I initiated step two with Vikram by my side: contacting major Indian wind turbine manufacturers, in the hope that one of them would sign a contract to build turbines for our business. As a customer with no money of his own, I was not surprised when all my letters went unanswered.

After much persistence I finally landed a meeting with Tulsi Tanti, the founder of a wind turbine manufacturing company called Suzlon. At the time, Suzlon was a multi-billion-dollar global company, and dominated the market in India. Tulsi Tanti himself was an extremely well-regarded entrepreneur in the country, and someone whom I looked up to. Tanti exuded the air of a man of homespun wisdom and inner strength. He had this special ability to distil complex arguments into simple messages, and radiated a calm confidence that left his listeners enthralled.

Worn down by my persistence, Tanti finally replied to my emails. He said he was attending an international climate conference and could meet me for only one hour in the lounge of Copenhagen airport.

I remember waiting for him at the airport, having flown in just for this one-hour opportunity. The large glass windows of the lounge revealed a city already dark by early afternoon, cloaked in the bitter cold of northern Europe. Tanti arrived with five or six of his entourage, ordered a tea and settled into the seat across from me. His eyes seemed to say, *Well, go on, then.*

My pitch to him was that the renewables industry in India was changing. The accelerated depreciation structure that had shaped the industry for the past decade was bound to evolve. Even though Suzlon was doing very good business under the current scheme, they should also prepare themselves for the coming revolution, where renewables assets in India would be operated by independent power producers, much like the company I was trying to build. Rather than having a bunch of passive owners buying up small stakes in renewables for a tax cut, we would have an industry of proper utility companies, operating renewable assets at massive scale. For these reasons he should sign a contract to sell turbines to me, one of the first Indian renewables utility companies in the making, at a discount.

'To you, I should be seen as a new customer,' I repeated. 'If I succeed in building this business, I may very well be your biggest customer in a few years' time. If I do not succeed, then you lose nothing. We can simply tear up the agreement between us. It's just a piece of paper, after all.'

Tanti paused and considered this carefully. Then he said, 'If it is true, and the industry does shift, then why should *you* be the person that I trust to pull this off?'

I tried to buy myself some time as I chose my words carefully. Finally, after some thought, I replied: 'You have to put your faith in someone.' I looked at him straight in the eyes as I said this. *Look into my eyes. I want to build the most innovative renewables company that India has ever seen.*

Although I didn't say this aloud, I was secretly hoping that my association with the Caparo Group would made my claims much more plausible. It could also ease Tanti's worries about whether I could pay for the turbines I was asking for. What he didn't know was the nature of the association – and I intended to keep it that way.

Tanti looked at me from the corner of his eyes. The air between us appeared like a tightrope to me, and I could hear the clocks in the airport lounge, each denoting the time in various cities across the world.

'I'll think about it,' Tanti replied.

In a few months' time, we had negotiated a contract stipulating that I would be able to purchase $1 billion's worth of wind turbines from him. This was the first development that turned the business from an idea into a real possibility.

The third and final step, though, was the most crucial: financing. How would we raise money for this business, now that we had a reputable brand as well as a vendor contract? How could we convince investors that we had a viable business idea, even though we had not built a single windmill?

Vikram and I spent two months tirelessly drawing up various models and possibilities while perfecting our pitch. He was an incredibly fast learner, which only encouraged me to shoot for the moon. We drew up a gruelling investor roadshow schedule: 300 meetings in the span of forty days. These meetings spanned many geographies, from London to New York, Houston, Hong Kong, Singapore and Geneva.

One of our earliest meetings was with a famous hedge fund in London. It was said that getting into the good grace of the managing director could have rippling effects across the investment world. Vikram was noticeably nervous before the meeting, tapping his pen on his knuckle while we waited for nearly an hour. I repeatedly went over my notes about the director – the most important part of a pitch, I often said, is knowing whom you're selling to – and summoned all my energy.

Usually an entrepreneur would need to prove that an idea is viable before bringing it before such big investors. I knew that what we were attempting would be the hardest sell of all, since we had no proof of concept but just an idea and a revolutionary prediction about the future of a complicated industry in India.

During the first three minutes of our presentation the director's eyes did not even look up at me: they were scanning the introductory brief on his desk with a quick intensity. After the fourth minute, he held up his hand to stop me mid-sentence.

'Ravi, hold on a minute.' I stopped and looked up expectantly.

'Let me get this straight,' he continued, 'You are putting no money of your own in this company, correct?'

'Correct.'

'But you want to be the majority owner.'

'Correct.' I could see where this was going.

'But you have no assets on the ground. You have built nothing.'

'Correct.'

'And you have no experience in energy, let alone renewable energy. You have no certainty that the industry will change in the way you think it will.'

'Correct.'

'And you have only three employees.'

'Four, if you include the receptionist.'

The director stood up to shake my hand.

'Gentlemen, I apologize, but I am quite busy, and I am sure you can find your way out.'

9

GOING PUBLIC

❧

I ALWAYS say that 12 October 2010 is Mytrah's founding day. That cold and dreary morning, I made my way to the London Stock Exchange at 10 Paternoster Row with Vikram, Helen and other family members. It was just two months after the meeting with the hedge fund manager who showed us the door.

The square was flanked on each side by formidable glass buildings. We walked onto the main floor of the stock exchange and were immediately greeted by the head of the Exchange.

'Welcome.' He shook our hands warmly. 'We're very excited to have you here for the opening bell.' Although, I was soon to learn that, unlike in New York, there is no actual bell at the London Stock Exchange.

'Are you serious?' I kept whispering to Helen. 'There's no bell?' She chuckled into her hand, trying to avoid being seen as my co-conspirator.

We waited eagerly for the stock exchange to open at 8 a.m. sharp. My family, all wired up with anticipatory nervousness and excitement, looked around. Those three minutes may have been the longest minutes of my life.

At 7.58 a.m., Mytrah was still an idea. Then one minute passed. Two minutes passed. When the enormous digital clock on the wall hit 8 a.m., the trading floor instantaneously transformed into a hive of activity.

At 8.01 a.m., Mytrah became the world's first startup utility officially listed on the London Stock Exchange. All Vikram and I used to achieve this was the vendor contract from Suzlon, $10,000 of incorporation costs, and some imagination in selling our story. In just three minutes, we added $80 million of equity for a company valuation of more than $300 million.

The path leading to this moment was checkered with potholes and diversions, victories and many, many defeats. Out of the 300 investors we met over the past months, only ten agreed to a second meeting and only five actually invested. Yet we made a good case with those final five, and together they invested the entire $80 million that became our equity.

Entrepreneurs focus on the victories, but they rarely reveal just how messy and uncertain the process of building a company can be. I felt it was almost akin to my travels to Indian villages. There was never any straight highway to travel on. You had to look for diversions and U-turns on small local roads and sometimes, when the local road disappeared, you needed to rely on the good grace of farmers, who took you on their tractors through their fields to the other side.

We were now on the other side. I kissed Helen and hugged Vikram. This was going to be a different company from any other I had built.

———

Once the immediate exuberance of the IPO faded, I experienced a strange, bittersweet sensation, similar to what I had felt when first leaving Vipassana at Nagarjunasagar.

As entrepreneurs, we had 'won the game', or at least the first round of it. With just an idea, we had raised $80 million for a 26 per cent stake in Mytrah, creating a business valued at over $300 million. The sponsors' share of Mytrah's value, or my stake in it, was significant. Little did I know that over the next seven years or so the company would grow faster than I had ever anticipated, building out 2,000 megawatts of renewable energy assets. I had only put $10,000 in Mytrah, and if I had kept my shares as personal wealth, the IPO would have made me a paper billionaire in less than a decade.

Despite all this, as the adrenaline rush from the victory of the IPO fizzled out, I was once again caught in the cognitive dissonance of the moment. On the one hand I was deeply proud of our success, especially of Vikram's role. On the other hand, I was wracked by self-doubt and unease, a discomfort that persisted in the back of my mind. Both Vikram and I had put in a full year of hard work into the planning, execution and orchestration that had led to this moment. Yet, at the end of the day, our main strength had been in selling an idea, creating a narrative that drew people in.

How could our work justify these rewards? What value had I actually created in society? And whatever I did, how could it justify such a massive prize, a kind of personal wealth that most people in the world could never even imagine? It was a stark reminder of what I had really set out to do: to build a business that created value for a community of people who were usually barred from such rewards.

For most entrepreneurs, the common-sense understanding is that new businesses create value automatically. This is the second assumption of the myth of the entrepreneur: that by bringing an innovative idea, product or service to the market, an entrepreneur automatically creates value in the world.

Traditionally, this value is viewed in three ways. First, it is viewed for its innovation. Entrepreneurial ventures address unmet needs in the market, and in the face of competition each venture must bring innovative new products to consumers, which encourages more competition and increases productivity. Even when entrepreneurs destroy elements of the social or economic fabric, such as when their new technology upends an older industry, this 'creative destruction' eventually promotes progress.

Secondly, entrepreneurs are viewed as creating social value by generating employment. All businesses require some factor of human labour, and offering opportunities to the labour force is a crucial way in which businesses provide social good. Since labour, in theory, is a scarce (non-infinite) resource, businesses need to attract workers with competitive salaries or other benefits, thus spreading wealth and benefits across the population.

Lastly, entrepreneurs are viewed as engines of wealth creation. By seeking investments and by building and growing businesses, entrepreneurs create wealth not only for themselves, but also for investors, shareholders and employees. This wealth creation bolsters general economic growth, which trickles down to positively impact the many.

———

In all my earlier ventures, I had strongly believed that by simply creating my companies I was already fulfilling my obligations to society or creating 'value' in these ways. Therefore, I had only tinkered with the issues of inequality or social issues at the margins – for instance, by making sure to hire employees without a religious or gender bias. Yet, the consideration of how to *actively* create social value beyond the automatic functions of business was not something I had thought about deeply. Social value, I thought, would be created intrinsically within the entrepreneurial process.

But, as I mentioned in the previous chapter, this is an incomplete and passive understanding of value creation. Although I cannot deny that entrepreneurial ventures do generate value through innovation, employment and creation of wealth, most of us fail to recognize the potential value that has been left out of the process.

The danger in believing in automatic value creation is that it justifies dismantling everything that stands in the way of entrepreneurial innovation, sometimes to the incredible detriment of society at large. We must move from a common-sense understanding of value creation to something that cuts to the heart of the matter. As anthropologist David Harvey writes, 'Common sense is constructed out of longstanding practices of cultural socialization … It is not the same as the 'good sense' that can be constructed out of critical engagement with the issues of the day.'[1]

By dissecting the myth of the entrepreneur, i want to move the conversation from a common-sense understanding to a 'good sense' understanding that can be both charitable *and* critical of the role of the entrepreneur. Much of the contemporary 'entrepreneurial ecosystem' has been born because of the significant shift in consensus about how the global economy should work. Initially, this shift was fought in the battleground of ideas. Specifically, in the 1970s, a theory of the capitalist economy developed, largely as a reaction against two other competing models. The first was the model of Marxism and socialism, championed by the Soviet Union and its allies, and the second the model of state planning, intervention and welfare systems, which was common among the post-World War II capitalist countries.

Influenced by the central planning and production coordination required by the war, many post-WWII economies continued to operate as a mixture of free market forces and substantial government intervention, especially in fiscal and monetary policy. Public goods, such as healthcare and education, were viewed as the domain of the state. With two world wars and the Great Depression still fresh in the collective memory, it seemed natural that the 'free market' should not be left alone to its devices or seen as the sole provider of human well-being.

In the 1970s, however, a competing theory took hold. Supported by the writings of a group of economists at the University of Chicago, this theory championed a resurgence of laissez-faire ('hands off') economics.[2] Free trade, strong private property rights and free markets were suddenly seen as the best promoters of social well-being and economic growth. All government intervention and planning, on the other hand, was seen as an unfair infringement upon the free market.

According to the Chicago School, this type of market fundamentalism would not only usher in a strong global economy, but also 'liberate' individual entrepreneurial freedom and skills. This is not an *economic* claim but an *ethical* claim, expressing the belief that individual 'freedom' is the main source of social good, and that such social good could be maximized only by expanding the reach and frequency of free market transactions. Once entrepreneurs were 'liberated', they could add value to society through the aforementioned channels of wealth creation, employment and innovation.

Freedom meant individual freedom, which meant free enterprise. This idea sowed the seeds for a massive reorganization of the economic rules of the world. Starting from the developed world and slowly spreading unevenly across the developing world, laissez-faire economics became the norm in many places. Corporate interests saw it (rightly) as a kind of thinking that would work in their favour. Think tanks such as the Institute of Economic Affairs in London and the Heritage Foundation in Washington D.C. began lobbying governments with Chicago-flavoured policies. The institutions responsible for world governance and international relations in the post-war era, namely the International Monetary Fund, the World Bank, the World Trade Organization and the Bank of International Settlements, were heavily influenced by such economic theories.

Finally, the two most advanced economies in the world – the United Kingdom and the United States – had elected leaders, Margaret Thatcher and Ronald Reagan, who were fully on-board with this type of laissez-faire economics. This meant pushing for liberalization of the developing economies for open trade and wide-scale implementation of policies like deregulation across industries (most intensely in the financial industry), privatization of public industries, undoing of social welfare programmes, promotion of free trade and lower taxes on corporations.[3]

The bottom line of the 'neoliberal turn' of the 1970s was this: governments and the major unelected international bodies (like the IMF and the World Bank) implemented global policies based on the philosophy that entrepreneurial innovation needed to be 'freed' from the constraints and choke-holds of government intervention and basically anything else that stood in its way.[4]

———

The part of the story that is not told by entrepreneurs and corporate interests is that freedom for business did not mean freedom for everyone. Liberalized economies were not better equipped to take care of their populations than other models, such as the Nordic welfare states. Similarly, there were internal contradictions in the claim of achieving freedom through the free market; workers in economies with such policies, for instance, were significantly less free to organize into unions and bargain for better wages or working conditions.

As the famed Hungarian philosopher and political economist Karl Polanyi once wrote, the positive freedoms we earn from a free market also come attached with negative freedoms. While we are enjoying free trade, free enterprise, free speech and freedom of association, we are opening the doors to undesirable freedoms. For instance, through the dominance of laissez-faire economics, we also gain, Polanyi writes, 'the freedom to make inordinate gains without commensurable service to the community' (a negative freedom about which I felt very strongly those moments after Mytrah's IPO). Similarly, we allow for 'the freedom to keep technological inventions from being used for public benefit'. And lastly, we open the doors to 'the freedom to profit from public calamities'.

From the pharmaceutical industry hiking prices to oil and gas companies covering up evidence of global warming to the housing crisis of 2008, examples of these 'negative freedoms' exercised in our global economy are quite extensive. Those who gained from the positive freedoms of laissez-faire economies were largely entrepreneurs, corporate managers and financiers. Those who lost from the negative freedoms were everyday people.

In 2017, I was invited by the US State Department to attend their annual Global Entrepreneurship Summit, which happened to be held in Hyderabad. The annual theme was 'Women First, Prosperity for All', and it was a sight to behold: 1,500 leading entrepreneurs from around the world, more than half of them women, packed into a convention centre in downtown Hyderabad. You could nearly taste the buzz of energy in the air, and I felt a swell of pride in my heart that my hometown had been chosen as the meeting ground for such an event.

Since I was known in the business world as the founder and chairman of a major renewable energy company, I was listed on various panels and talks to debate the future of energy. But I specifically asked to be added to a panel called 'The Entrepreneurial Ecosystem'. I was seated next to the CEO of Digital Finance Institute, the head of Bain India, and a director from the US Department of Labor. It was going to be an interesting conversation, I thought to myself.

Usually, when entrepreneurs are pushed to talk about the 'entrepreneurial ecosystem', the kind of laissez-faire market fundamentalism I have outlined above looks pretty good. Which entrepreneur does not want deregulation, lower taxes and privatization? After all, I myself had capitalized on many of these developments throughout my career. Indeed, it had become instinctive to argue that since entrepreneurs provide enormous value by the nature of their activity, nothing should constrain them. On these panels, entrepreneurs usually talked about how to dismantle cumbersome government policies, or how to spark privatization in some inefficient public industry.

When it was time for my opening remarks on the panel, my palms were sweating. It was not the best platform on which to be talking about some of my ideas, and as much as I held on to my convictions, I was worried about offending the other panelists – or worse, the audience. I had learned that antagonizing my peers was not the right strategy, but could I strike that balance and communicate the need for principled agency?

'Instead of thinking about how to build an entrepreneurial ecosystem fit for *us*,' I opened shakily, 'perhaps we should think about how entrepreneurs could build an ecosystem that better serves society. We hold so many of these conferences, where we bring together brilliant and creative entrepreneurs, that it becomes too natural to talk as if everything should revolve around *us* as a group. But maybe' – here I glanced at my fellow panel members – 'that is not the way to build the most flourishing society.'

To my surprise, Amit Chandra, the managing director at Bain India, quickly agreed with me. 'I will second Ravi on that,' he said in a cheerful tone.

I continued ahead, bolstered by this unanticipated alliance. 'Entrepreneurs do create value in the world, but we have to reconsider and rethink the context in which we do so. Sometimes, perhaps we may need to stomach some inconveniences in order to ensure a more equitable or fair world. Other times, we should be bold enough to experiment with new ways of creating value, by redistributing wealth, taking care of our work forces beyond what is legally required, and contributing to the ecosystem or communities in which our businesses operate. These should be the first things we do, not the last, although history has seemed to work in the opposite direction.'

After the panel I shook Amit's hand with genuine warmth. We locked eyes, and there was an energy that passed between us, like those of kindred spirits.

'Are you familiar with Ashoka?' he asked me in a whispering tone.

I knew he was a prominent king in Indian history and that his symbol, the chakra, was incorporated as part of the Indian national flag. Beyond that I had not read about him since childhood.

'A bit of general knowledge, but not much, to be honest,' I admitted to Amit.

'Take a look at some of his writings if you have a chance. I think you try to share in his spirit, which I commend.'

When I went home that evening I dug out an old book of mine on Ashoka's life. Amit's words had stuck with me, and I wanted to refresh my knowledge of what I had learnt about the emperor in school. What I rediscovered was a story of remarkable trans-valuation, the story of a king who completely revolutionized what it meant to create value for society.

Ashoka was the third emperor of the Maurya dynasty in India, a ruler of immense power, who inherited one of the largest empires in ancient India from his grandfather, the legendary Chandragupta. When he first began his reign, Ashoka was like any traditional Indian ruler; he rigorously followed the approach of the *Arthaśāstra*, a treatise which laid out hundreds of rules and recommendations for monarchs, from how the palace should be laid out to what provisions the ruler should make for defence, advisors, diplomacy, and so on. The *Arthaśāstra* defined the value of traditional kingship as strong government, strong military, and loyalty of the peoples. The sign of a good and worthy king was conquest, the obedience he commanded, and wealth.

Ashoka excelled as a traditional king. But in the eighth year of his coronation he faced his biggest challenge. Kalinga, a distant state that none of Ashoka's ancestors had successfully conquered, staged a rebellion, and it was now the king's duty to quell the uprising. But the people of Kalinga were proud warriors, and an infamous and bloody conflict ensued, leaving 100,000 fighters and civilians dead, and perhaps 150,000 deported to the wild terrain outside the city-state. The entire area was plundered and destroyed, and Ashoka watched with his own eyes the destruction of the fertile lands of Kalinga as it blazed with fire.

This moment of victory was the most definitive of Ashoka's life. A lesser king might have been filled with pride, but Ashoka was left haunted by the bloodshed he had witnessed. He had seen the death and destruction of people and Mother Earth: did the value of conquest justify this? In a sudden flash of conscience, Ashoka is said to have looked out at the barren ruins of Kalinga and experienced a heart-wrenching awakening.

This set Ashoka on a search for ways to understand and express his inner revolution. He converted to Buddhism, immersing himself in the pious study of Buddhist dhamma. Yet he was not an enforcer of his religious faith – India was still largely Hindu, and Ashoka saw all religions as being part of the same project: the promotion of a righteous and ethical way of life. He did not force his Buddhist beliefs on anyone else and encouraged religions to coexist in harmony.

Rather than seek power through expanding his empire, Ashoka renounced conquest altogether after Kalinga. The only thing he wanted from his neighbours, he proclaimed, was for them not to live in fear of aggression – a shocking deviation from the idea of kinghood as being valued by conquest, especially for those times. Ashoka felt that by eliminating conquest and bloodshed, he could focus on his real purpose, the *real value* of a king, which was to promote the moral uplift and happiness of his people. To this end he began a pan-India reform movement, and spent his time on efforts such as building public works, weeding out corruption amongst civil servants, instating fair wages, granting relief to prisoners on death row, and advocating animal rights.

Ashoka was an example of an individual who was not afraid to question the values he had inherited about how to be a king and ruler. He was open to reflection and to translating that reflection into real change. In governing as he did, he cast aside all the things kings before him believed were valuable.

Instead, he sought to find value in his people. To Ashoka, the duty of the king was to 'repay the debt he owed to all beings' (Edict 22).

It was the idea of such a debt that surfaced in me through the experience and practice of Vipassana, and I knew its repayment would continue long beyond my own life.

10

TRUSTEESHIP

———◆❋◆———

THE Mytrah initial public offering (IPO) unleashed a tornado of activity. With this injection of capital, Vikram and I now needed to turn the idea we had sold to investors into a functioning company. Some of these processes were already set in motion and just needed our signal to move full steam ahead. Others were still decisions in the making. And others were held up by the usual obstacles – unexpected delays, unresponsive partners, slow government approvals … the whole lot of contingencies.

I knew from the very beginning that I did not want to be the centre of Mytrah's operations. I aimed to disengage from the day-to-day business of the company. My job would be to offer long-term strategic guidance and serve as its external face for the investors, who tended to prefer people with greying hair. By stepping back, I could also keep my mind clear and uncluttered for the few decisions each year that reckoned with the company's long-term future. The operations of Mytrah and its immediate growth were left to Vikram and his leadership team.

My role at Mytrah, just like my personal story in this book, was akin to that of a grain of sand in an oyster. For a pearl is a jewel formed around a grain of sand. That grain of sand serves as its initial seed, catalysing the pearl into being. Once the final, beautiful form of the pearl itself has grown around it, the seed loses its identity as the initial grain. In fact, the grain of sand is then only significant in its *absence*.

I made a very conscious decision to be a grain of sand for Mytrah. In 2011, roughly ten months after our IPO, I named Vikram the managing director and CEO of Mytrah. Having worked with him for two years I was already firmly convinced about his abilities. Vikram was a natural leader who did not fumble under pressure. Even though there were still some rough edges, he was bold and daring, and he had a mind that could assess risk with startling accuracy. Even though I had strong lifelong objections to hiring family members, Vikram had still gained his position by merit; if anything, I judged him more harshly because he was family, and he had to prove himself over and beyond an outsider would have been required to in order to stifle any rumours of favouritism on my part.

Of course, the decision made waves in the company. Top management, most of whom had spent more time in the infrastructure industry than the total years of Vikram's age, would now directly report to this brazen, fast-talking twenty-eight-year-old. A transition of this kind required a strong message to be sent with it, so after the announcement I spent more and more time in London, making only infrequent visits to Hyderabad. If people from the company sent me emails on matters that were supposed to be under Vikram's purview, I forwarded them to him without any response.

Many in the company found this extremely odd. In India it was well known that the 'father' of the company traditionally held control for a long time, controlling his successors for decades. I was forty-five when I ceded control to Vikram, and when I said I wanted to let go, I really did.

Before I left for London, I sat with Vikram in his corner office. We looked out towards the high-rises of Gachibowli, which had been just parched agricultural land a mere twenty years ago. It was a surreal feeling – twenty years ago, our family and our city could not have imagined the things we now called memories.

I felt the overwhelming and bittersweet tenderness of a parent who knows he needs to let go but is also gripped by the intense, irrational desire to stay, to impart knowledge, to protect. Yet this was impossible. My own father's greatest gift to me was freedom, the severing of my desire to identify with him. I looked out into the sun so he would not see the tears in my eyes.

'So much has changed, hasn't it?' I asked, surprised by my own wistful tone.

'Yes, Ravi.'

'You must have faith in yourself. I know I do.'

Vikram shifted in his seat. 'I hope I do not let you down.'

'You have never let me down. And you won't this time.' What I thought in my mind was: it is my honour and karma to have even crossed paths with such a human being.

I made one last promise to Vikram: I would not call him to check on him, however curious I was or dire the situation. But I would respond if he ever called me.

It was perhaps the best decision I ever made for the company.

Life for me became an unexpected and beautiful duality. While Mytrah blossomed under the leadership team with Vikram at the helm, Helen and I led our own life in the quietude of south London, halfway across the globe. We went to Sainsbury's and bought photo frames for the house, which we filled with various memories: the Kilimanjaro hike where we met, our visit to the Taj Mahal with the kids, a shot of her eating ice cream in Vienna. We planned outings and eagerly awaited Daman and Aditi's time back home from school.

Most of the days, Helen and I simply sat in silence in opposite ends of the apartment. Helen would be hunched over her laptop – even though she was technically 'retired', she still insisted on maintaining a razor-sharp understanding of her industry and often spent a few hours a day reading scientific papers and news releases. I browsed through the *Economist* or stared out the window at the Thames.

There was a mute shock to it all, a sense that I had abstracted from the world and stripped life of everything besides the necessities, only to discover that by eliminating the desires and aversions of my own ego, I had, conversely, got everything I had ever wanted.

———

A year after the IPO I decided it was time to put the second phase of my plan into action. Enough time had passed, the dust had settled, and the company had stabilized after its initial years of growing pains. So, I was sitting at home in Fulham and thinking about how to find the right person to aid me in this next phase. The first link of my search results on Google led to a peer-reviewed ranking of lawyers in various categories. Under the category I was looking for, I found the name – John Riches, Withers LLP.

My first meeting with John took place at the Withers office on Old Bailey Street. There was something quaint about that area of London, something that exuded a sense of history and stateliness. I entered and took a seat in the glossy reception room, which was filled with men in pinstripe suits and their assistants.

John greeted me and then led me to his office. He was not very tall, but lean like a runner, with salt-and-pepper hair and rectangular glasses. He waited for me to get comfortable before starting. 'So, Ravi, do you know what it is that I do?'

I responded honestly. 'You were the first result that came up when I Googled, "best trust lawyer in the world".'

John laughed. 'That's one way of doing it.' I took an immediate liking to him. He had a firm but easy way of speaking, and most importantly, when I looked into his eyes, I could see a gentle kindness. He seemed like someone who would hear me out.

'And a trust lawyer facilitates the establishment of trusts. From what I gather, trusts are essentially custodians of wealth.'

'That's a very good way of putting it, Ravi. You are right that trusts are legal custodians of wealth. But that is not exactly what I do. My job is really working with individuals and families who require wealth management, especially in the long term. Sometimes a trust structure is the best strategy, sometimes it isn't. But the main purpose is to create a good structure and process for planning and transferring significant wealth across generations.'

In the next hour, I unashamedly picked John Riches's mind. His knowledge of intergenerational wealth transfer was encyclopaedic, having worked with a global and diverse clientele, from some of the most storied families in Europe to substantial new wealth-creators in Asia and the Middle East. He could extemporize about the particularities of inheritance in Saudi Arabia, the workings of the Indian business family and the history of the American estate tax, all in one breath. Even though he was careful to omit all details from his account, I could guess that in his thirty-year career he had witnessed, or had had his hand in, the planning and distribution of some of the greatest fortunes in the world.

Family wealth was a messy business, John warned, so planning was key. He had seen dynastic families fall apart. He had seen wills revealed, only to break families into factions that would not speak to each other for decades. He had seen structures that were made with good intentions become corrupted by people who were able to manipulate the system put in place; for example, one trustee who was the best friend of the original founder's son managed to alter the trust deed to give himself a significant and legally valid payoff. Wealth turned sister against brother, child against parent, founding family against management. It was something that needed to be handled with extreme care.

What John emphasized most in wealth planning was the importance of balancing principles with flexibility – too much of the former could mean an overly rigid structure that did not adapt to changing circumstances, while too much of the latter could leave you vulnerable to bad actors who could take advantage of loopholes and obscurities.

I tried to absorb all the information that was now swirling around in my head. After a while, John looked at me with a puzzled expression. 'Not everyone is so interested in the history and theory behind these things, you know. They just want me to set up something that minimizes taxes and distributes their money to their children.'

It was my turn to laugh. His suspicion was endearing. 'It's very interesting, John, and the more I know, the better.'

John nodded approvingly. 'So, after hearing my entire schtick, what do you think? What is *your* purpose? I assume you are a wealthy man who wants to set a plan. So, what can I do for you?'

I told John what I wanted to do. It was something I had thought about for a long time. When I was finished, John looked at me with an even more puzzled expression.

'Are you sure about this?' was the first thing he asked, after a long pause.

'Yes, I am sure.'

'You understand that establishing a trust is irrevocable, right? Any decision you make, once you make it, can never be undone. The way you set it up on day one will be the way it works possibly indefinitely.'

'I understand.'

'I thought so – it seems like you did plenty of research yourself!' He seemed excited, and rocked in his chair. 'So, let me get this straight. You want to entrust 90 per cent of your shares in your company, Mytrah, to a charitable trust. And you want to set up this charitable trust so that it focuses on development goals in India.'

'If enough wealth is generated, we could perhaps look at other countries too. But the scale of need in India is enormous. I would like to pick some key areas to focus on in the next few years, like women's education.'

'Understood. But Mytrah was just set up a few months ago.'

'Yes.'

'So, you have no idea what this wealth will be in the future, since you have no idea how much the company will grow.'

'Yes.'

'In essence, you're donating a fortune of unknown size to a charitable trust.'

'I suppose you could put it that way.'

'I see,' John said, although I could tell he was still sceptical. 'How old are you again?'

'I'm forty-five now, turning forty-six.'

John nodded slowly. 'It's quite rare for wealth creators to think about philanthropy so early on, especially for Asian entrepreneurs. At least in my experience. On top of that, you have no idea how much this is going to be worth in the future. What if it is billions of dollars, and you have to give it all away because you cannot amend the trust? What if it is much less, and you have the opposite problem of not being able to take care of your family, if the 10 per cent you set aside for them is not enough?'

These were important and valid questions. At the same time, I realized that John and I were approaching the problem from different points of view. I did not consider this an act of philanthropy for various reasons, reasons that would illuminate the gap in understanding between us.

John had worked with plenty of wealth creators, many of whom went on to become prominent philanthropists. As I saw it, my decision stemmed from a different set of beliefs and assumptions about the world.

Don't get me wrong, I admired and learned a lot from many philanthropically engaged entrepreneurs and leaders. I salute the Giving Pledge, the Buffet-Gates initiative urging billionaires to pledge half their wealth to charity in their lifetime, a public campaign that has steered the conversation about wealth towards social responsibility and the importance of giving back. And I could not help but admire Bill Gates, who chose to apply his mind and time full-time to philanthropic pursuits in the prime of his career, while so many entrepreneurs, myself included, found it hard to step back from business even though they may be desperately needed elsewhere.

But I had also seen an uglier side of philanthropy that made me unable to believe that it was the optimal method of redirecting wealth to the right beneficiaries. The core issue was this: in most cases, acts of philanthropy were not based on displacement of the giver's ego, shifting the focus to collective welfare, but were tightly bound to the individual's ego, feeding it rather than setting it aside.

Time and again I have witnessed philanthropy being used as a means for individual reinvention or legacy creation. I have sat at galas, charity balls and fundraisers where entrepreneurs who made their fortunes in unscrupulous sectors employing unscrupulous practices were applauded for giving away some increment of their wealth. Identities morph with alarming speed in such rites of repentance, and wealth creators who were disliked for decades become rebranded as magnanimous philanthropists overnight. This kind of philanthropy is predominantly driven by a desire to immortalize one's name, not by a genuine dedication to social impact.

Simultaneously, among the philanthropists whose primary focus *is* social impact, I encountered more and more wealth creators and entrepreneurs who believed they could do a better job than governments or other social institutions in cracking the problems of the world. Among the wealthiest set in society, having your own philanthropic foundation became a coveted status symbol, something that proved you were a true leader 'changing the world'.

These believers in 'philanthro-capitalism' did not like to focus on how philanthropic foundations are bodies with little oversight, known for their historically high administration costs, and for their lack of good metrics for measuring impact. Nor did they like to be pointed out that there is personal bias in their allocation of resources, which sees money being poured into the hobbies or passions of the foundation leaders (e.g., fine arts education in countries with globally low literacy rates, treatment of a rare disease affecting a member of the founding family, or horse-racing). I would not like to suggest that these campaigns do not create positive impact, but we cannot ignore that the *process* of capital allocation is still tightly controlled by the personal preferences of the wealth creators versus the needs of the community at large.

I think the key difference between philanthropy versus championing other structural forms of redistribution lies in the answers to the following questions: What do we earn? What do we deserve? And what can we *own* as individuals? The myth of the entrepreneur is supported by the belief in meritocracy and deservedness, the idea that individual entrepreneurs earned their wealth because of their innately superior intelligence or merit. Since they earned their success through merit, their skill-set makes them the best-suited candidates to make decisions for society, not just in business, but in global development and social issues such as poverty, poor sanitation and water scarcity.

Taxes, the redistribution mechanism by which wealth was redirected towards public goods through an elected political body, constituted the 'stealing' of money by government. Private foundations, on the other hand, which were tax-exempt and led by billionaire-philanthropists, could sidestep the government and solve the issues of the world. Underlying all this was the subtle, unspoken belief that wealth-creating entrepreneurs, as the most intelligent and talented individuals in society, knew best.

While it is very admirable for talented wealth creators to take up social and other issues, relying on philanthropy turns a structural issue into an individualist one. The underlying contradictions in our society are systemic and institutional. Expecting a collection of individuals to change that through their personal efforts can mean that we fail to imagine a wholly different society, where the basic relations and organizations in the world are reconfigured.

An even more worrisome trend arising from this belief in meritocracy is that it becomes a self-justification for entrepreneurs and wealth creators who do *not* participate in philanthropy on any significant scale, or do not view their extraordinary wealth as anything that demands responsibility to greater society.

I heard this refrain so often in my discussions with entrepreneurs, especially in India: 'I built my company from nothing. If I can do it, then so can others.' It's a meritocratic playing field, and so it's not *my* responsibility to help where others end up. The assumption of meritocracy is used as a reason by entrepreneurial wealth creators to justify inequality. Indeed, the standard entrepreneurs' sense of meritocratic achievement, plus their relative social isolation – as they only operate among their own class – make for a dangerous combination when they try to empathize with the less fortunate or attempt to understand how the system through which they achieved success is skewed.

The problem with a blanket belief in meritocracy is twofold. One, there is simply no level playing field. The idea that 'anyone can become somebody' must be viewed in the light of the fact that the greatest predictors of success in many entrepreneurs' lives are inherited or unrelated to their personal efforts.

Being born in a place with relative stability, infrastructure and access to education, for instance, are critical determinants of future success. Having educated or entrepreneurial parents also boost one's chances significantly. There can be no presumption of equal opportunity between the starting points of modern-day entrepreneurs, many of whom come from middle-class backgrounds in the developed countries, or from privileged circles in the developing countries, and a child in a war-torn or completely undeveloped economy.

For much of my life I overlooked the less visible privileges of my own background. My father was someone who worked his way up from nothing. He grew up in a slum in Hyderabad, housed in one room with nine of his siblings. By the time I was born he had improved our quality of life to that of a lower-middle-class family. We lived in a rental home and did not own a car. My father came home after work with the little bit of rice and dal that would be cooked for dinner that evening.

By the time I was ten my father had made his first strides in entrepreneurship, expanding his operations from a gas station to a transportation business and, finally, a distillery and sugar factory, both esteemed industries in India. Within a decade he grew from working for himself to having hundreds of employees working for him. When I turned eleven we moved to our first family home, which was built on a beautiful, shaded plot of land in Tarnaka. My mother hired a driver and a cook, and we began life with the trappings of a family with more means.

The kind of 'meritocratic' advancement my family enjoyed allowed me to assume that social mobility was generally possible. Since I never took over my father's businesses or utilized his funds, I believed that, for all intents and purposes, I was making wealth on my own. While I was trying to separate myself from the more obvious privileges, in hindsight I realize I was still building on the back of decades of material comfort, education, mentorship, connections and other intangible resources. I started with far, far more than a blank slate.

Not only is there no such thing as equal opportunity across the world, but extreme inequality *erodes* whatever meritocracy or equal opportunity we do have, which self-perpetuates a cycle of worsening inequality. Rent-seeking, the process through which those in positions of wealth and power alter the rules of the economy to further benefit themselves, is believed to be one of the chief causes of sustained inequality.

In developing countries, the use of money to power and influence for its own favour is called out as corruption. India is filled with examples of business interests purchasing political cooperation through bribes and kickbacks. In developed countries, the same mechanism is at work, but operates in a regulated and legal framework of political campaign contributions, lobbyists and media companies. It is not called corruption, but in effect it is no different. Whether it is an envelope filled with cash given to a Hyderabadi government official or a property developer in San Francisco paying a lobbyist to pass a favourable bill, the result is the same: the already rich rewrite the rules of the game in their favour.

Michael Young, who was the first person to use and coin the term 'meritocracy' in his 1959 book, *The Rise of the Meritocracy*, wrote in a 2001 *Guardian* article that ' ... it is good sense to appoint individual people to jobs on their merit ... but it is the opposite when those who are judged to have merit of a particular kind harden into a new social class without room in it for others.'[1] The myth of the entrepreneur is guilty of using meritocracy to support exactly that hardened and exclusive social class.

All these thoughts ran in my mind as I prepared to meet John Riches. I could not change the practice of philanthropy, let alone the global economic system that produced this form of individualistic, imperfect redistribution. But perhaps I could take a personal step in the right direction, first by viewing my wealth not as a product of my achievement alone but as a result of my privileged access to opportunity, which meant I could not be an *owner* of wealth but simply a lucky *steward* of wealth.

The idea of holding surplus wealth in *trust* for the greater welfare of society has a long and storied history in India. The idea was popularized by Gandhi, who dreamed of an egalitarian society created, not out of violence, but from the moral reform and voluntary trusteeship of the wealthy.

To Gandhi, wealth did not belong to any individual. While every human being deserved the right to an honourable livelihood (a way to sustain oneself and one's family through honest means), every type of labour had to be rewarded materially in the same way. A businessman, an artist and a teacher should enjoy the same material recompense for their labour. Those who create surplus wealth should treat such wealth as belonging to the community and see it as something created for the sole purpose of enhancing the welfare of that community.

Gandhi's view of human nature was deeply optimistic – he believed that it was within all of us to reach a spiritual and ethical understanding that overcame greed or attachment to personal possessions. This way, inequality could be eradicated by moral reform and voluntary trusteeship. By convincing wealth creators to live like everyone else, and by entrusting all surplus wealth for the welfare of the community, we could transform into a more egalitarian society without the violence of a revolution.

Pure trusteeship, the belief in the stewardship of wealth and the rejection of personal ownership of wealth, is very different from the 'humane capitalism' that some entrepreneurs and business leaders advocate today. Indeed, as the destructive elements of profit-first enterprise become more obvious, and as the public (especially the youth) grows increasingly distrustful of the incentives and tactics of corporations, some business leaders are advocating that companies consider not only profits but other 'stakeholders' in business, such as people (especially employees) and the planet itself.

This 'triple-bottom-line,' as they call it, diverts some of the focus on profits to other means of producing value. Yet the efforts of humane capitalism, at least in my experience, are always *on the margins*, where some minimal percentage of wealth is redistributed for the collective good. My idea of trusteeship is the opposite: a minimal percentage of wealth should be left to the wealth creator, just enough for his modest subsistence, while everything else should be entrusted to advance the welfare of the greater society. If trusteeship is the real cure, 'humane capitalism' is a band-aid on a gushing wound.

When I was young, one of my favourite books was *The Creation of Wealth* by R.M. Lala. I must have read the book twenty times, bringing it with me to many of my afternoons in Golconda. The book documents the foundation and rise of the Tatas, one of the most reputable businesses families in India. Today the Tatas are a 100-billion-dollar conglomerate and their name is among the most well-known Indian brands in the world. They are also the best example of trusteeship in action.

The founder of the Tatas, Jamsetji Tata, built his empire on the foundational philosophy of trusteeship. For more than a hundred years now, the majority stakeholders in the Tata businesses have been the charitable trusts, which own about 66 per cent of the shares in the holding company of the Tata businesses. Moreover, every segment of the Tata empire, from steel to consulting services, was fashioned with an eye on creating not only financial value or profit, but *communal* value. The Tata steel plants built educational, health and community facilities for employees as early as in the nineteenth century.

Whenever disaster or misfortune struck an area near a Tata business, the company would proactively dedicate funds and manpower for relief. Since the inception of the Tata Trusts, Tata company profits have gone into constructing some of the greatest research, arts and higher-education institutions in India. The Tata trusts have also distributed funds to non-profit organizations tackling social issues around the world.

To Jamsetji Tata, creating value for a greater community defined entrepreneurship. 'In a free enterprise,' he said, 'the community is not just another stakeholder in business but is in fact the very purpose of its existence.'

In structuring my own trust, I learned from the strengths and weaknesses of the giants who came before me. Besides the Tatas, another example I admired was Atlantic Philanthropies, a foundation started by Chuck Feeney, the billionaire-founder of one of the largest duty-free businesses in the world. He entrusted his shares in the company, worth about $5.8 billion, to a charitable foundation very early in life.

Not only did Feeney live incredibly frugally after giving away all his wealth early in his lifetime, but he also never publicly disclosed his philanthropic activity until a lawsuit with a former business partner forced him to reveal his donations to the public. He decentred his ego entirely in the act of giving – he did not seek public attention for his altruism but was quiet about it, knowing that he did what was right.

I tried my best to follow Feeney's dedication to in-life giving. To that end I did not meet John Riches at the end of my life, but long before even the end of my entrepreneurial career. Moreover, I was entrusting an unknown amount of wealth to a charitable trust, before that wealth was even created. I would never have a public net worth, nor be known as a major wealth creator. I would be well-off, yes, but not inordinately wealthy, in the way the major philanthropists are, since almost all my stake in Mytrah had been pledged to a charitable trust from day one.

By entrusting my shares at the inception of the company, I was also changing the identity of the company itself. No matter what size Mytrah became, it would always be a company that was founded with an inextricable link to deliberate, collective value creation. Unknown to most people at Mytrah, they worked for a company where the majority of 'shareholder value' or profit would go into a charitable trust. The shares I entrusted would be worth more than 1 billion dollars by 2017. I only hope that they will be worth many, many more times that amount in the future decades.

Vikram stood by me through this entire process. He was still young, perhaps too young to have thought deeply about these questions. After all, I myself did not consider them until I was well into my forties. Still, one thing I must give him credit for is that he never once questioned my decision.

When we signed the official legal documents for The Pravaha Trust, he put one hand on my shoulder. 'How do you feel, Uncle?' he asked. 'It is a good thing you have done, giving all this away.'

'I am not giving anything away, Vikram. I am getting everything I ever wanted.'

I meant what I said. I truly did not feel as if I was giving anything away. Rather, I was 'correcting', for an amount of wealth that I should never have been given in the first place. In an ideal world, surplus wealth in anyone's hands would be automatically redirected towards the welfare of the greater community. I was not 'renouncing' wealth; I was redistributing rewards since the traditional systems of redistribution in my society, from what I could tell, were broken.

The experience of giving is not something that is only relevant to wealthy entrepreneurs. Far from it. In fact, plenty of people in the world with much less give much more, if we are to measure giving as a proportion of what one has. For most families, giving to others means *giving up* something for themselves, whether that is a night at a restaurant or a vacation for the family. The poor in India, who do not even have enough money to feed themselves, often give to create their own safety nets, putting a portion of their income into a collective pot that a member of the community can draw from in times of crisis. I was lucky to be able to give while knowing that I did not have to sacrifice anything – even with 90 per cent of the wealth in my name committed to charitable purposes there would be enough left over for me to live a very decent life.

The real lesson that I learned from this process was that human nature would always be prone to inertia, self-justification and ego. I could not trust that once Mytrah grew, I would not be affected by all the wealth that would suddenly be 'mine'. I could not promise that I would not change, the way I had seen others do, under the auspices of wealth and power. In order to set up Mytrah with the first principles of real value creation for greater society, I needed to make this decision from the very beginning.

I meditated often during this period, wherever I could – in the office, in the car, at home, and before I fell asleep at night. The reminder of impermanence, the experiential understanding of this, guided me and quieted any remaining doubts.

When I reflect on my decision to create the Pravaha Trust, I am torn by the knowledge that trusteeship is, for all intents and purposes, not a sustainable solution. Despite the teachings and influence of Gandhi, and the examples of major companies like the Tatas, we have not seen trusteeship bring about any redistribution of wealth on a major scale. My efforts too would be as only a few drops in the ocean, barely grazing the surface of global inequality.

The reason is that trusteeship, just like philanthropy, is an individualist solution to a systemic issue. Inequality has to do with the very basic organization of society, as codified by law and institutions. To upturn inequality, one would need institutional reforms – like changes in the global tax regime, provision of better access to education, allocation of greater resources for alleviation of poverty, or, if we are to take Scheidel's scepticism towards peaceful reform, wholesale revolution. Trusteeship, however, is not an institutional or systemic solution. In our current world, trusteeship is simply an individual decision, where a wealth-creating entrepreneur decides to 'abdicate' claims to personal wealth because he or she is moved by the philosophy of shared wealth.

Nothing guarantees that individual entrepreneurs, or those who end up with surplus wealth, will be exposed to experiences that promote their taking up the philosophy of trusteeship. On the other hand, there are many incentives in our current society to do the opposite, such as the fame that comes from accumulating mass individual fortunes. It is much easier to believe that the set of values, norms and institutional rules that organize our society are basically unchangeable than to take a position that goes against such a belief. Therefore it is not surprising that trusteeship has not caught on as a widespread model.

However, the Pravaha Trust is not the end goal or the final leg of this journey. Trusteeship is not the final solution; it is just the one that I was able to implement in my position as an entrepreneur and majority shareholder in a sizeable company. Yet, just as Mytrah was a vehicle that created wealth for the Pravaha Trust, I see the Trust acting as a grain of sand for a different entity altogether, an entity that will attempt to consolidate and share resources for social impact across India.

The problem is that current private efforts at social development in India are incredibly fragmented. A portion of the enormous fortunes of billionaires is channelled into family-run philanthropic foundations that are closely controlled and founder-centric. These foundations have significant resources and do good work, yet are essentially 'walled gardens' of isolated efforts that do not accept external funding and cannot address any issue in India on any significant scale. On the other end of the spectrum, tens of thousands of small-scale non-profit organizations contribute to India's development in their own way (India has the largest number of non-profit organizations in the world), yet most are crippled by poor governance, inefficient operations or lack of funding.

The scale of need in India is enormous, and the development shortfall in India amounts to trillions of dollars. In the next few decades the wealth created in India will also be enormous, with some projections claiming that India may be the largest economy in the world by 2050. The question then will be: how will that wealth be put to use? If people are moved to apply their wealth towards collective welfare, what kind of organizations can they donate to, or participate in, for maximum social impact? Rather than so many fragmented, disconnected efforts at social development, I think India could benefit from resource-sharing and knowledge-sharing across the many organizations operating within its borders.

What I have in mind is an open, collaborative foundation focusing on some of the biggest issues facing India today in education, health and sanitation. Rather than use the Pravaha Trust as a private foundation, I would like to hand over its funds to an independent and open foundation that solicits donations from *all* sections of society: from billionaires, corporations, the middle class, the poor, the Indian diaspora, and anyone else who may believe in a new India. If Pravaha donates a 'seed' of a billion of dollars to a foundation – which is called, say, Build India Foundation – which then goes out and tries to raise tens of billions of dollars from others, then for the first time we may have an organization capable of building some of the most ambitious and large-scale public infrastructure in India. Rather than a private foundation building ten or even 100 schools one by one, Build India Foundation should aim to build five schools in *every district* in India, thus creating an opportunity to also provide a completely new model of education for millions of children across the country.

My life has been a series of plans that people thought were too ambitious or just plain crazy. Yet, each time, good luck and the efforts of people far smarter and more talented than I turned every small seed into a flourishing reality. I intend to spend the next phase of my life focusing on getting the people and support necessary to set the stage for something like a Build India Foundation. Once this happens, the Pravaha Trust itself would transfer all its assets to the Foundation, then dissolve. I would disengage and let the talented, passionate people at this Build India Foundation utilize the funds as they believe will achieve the most impact in India. In giving, *ownership* must be inverted (much the way the ego must be decentred in Vipassana). We cannot hold on to and control what we give. We can only be a grain of sand.

I have no idea whether something like the Build India Foundation of my dreams can happen, and that even if it does, how long it would take to build. Yet I know I must try to build one.

———

In this book I critique an illness, an illness for which I offer no cure. For many years now, I have been concerned by the unequal rewards and outcomes within societies, differences that far exceed what is reasonable. There are theorists, academics and policymakers who have written much more and thought much harder about an exact diagnosis and cure for this disease. They are the people who have dedicated their lives to thinking about how to build a more equitable world, and can offer totalizing theories, research-driven policies and clear prescriptions.

I, on the other hand, cannot offer any policy, philosophical treatise or call to revolution that guarantees the world will change for the better. I can only offer what I know, which is insight gathered on the drifting path of a single entrepreneur who was led to question his own values. My attempt is just one. One imperfect solution. One life. One inquiry. One grain of sand.

Epilogue
CONTRADICTION

———✳———

O NE day, just before winter, during the golden hour before sunset, a stillness reigned in our home. Winter was incoming, turning the earth-toned autumn into a brittle grey, and the London sky grew heavy with darkness. It was just before the holiday season, which meant the storefronts twinkled with displays. From my window I could see a steady stream of cars and people hurrying home from work, shielding themselves from the cold.

They reminded me of the world in motion, close yet impossibly far from the silence that wrapped itself around our life like a cocoon. Over the years, Helen and I had settled into a quiet and happy life. We went out little, and kept few social engagements besides those with family and close friends. If anyone came to visit, they would find us sitting at home in the free pajamas we got from Emirates flights.

I spent most of my day walking around in the apartment with two hands clasped behind my back. The rhythm of pacing soothed me, smoothed the ridges of my mind. It had been already seven years since Mytrah's founding. Time had passed slowly at first, then quickly, compressing with age and routine until every year seemed like a blur, dotted with small pinpricks of the unexpected.

The seeds we had planted years ago had started to sprout. The Pravaha Trust had begun distributing its first batch of funds, experimenting with small-scale social initiatives that could be expanded into national projects, such as a sports academy and an educational centre in a Hyderabad slum preparing at-risk adolescent girls for secondary school.

In the meantime, Mytrah's business itself was growing beyond our wildest expectations. There were victories and crises with every quarter – land acquisition problems in our new solar division, a big refinancing deal with a major pension fund, the hiring of hundreds more employees. Vikram flourished, and was able to lead the company while being a family man to his wife and daughter, something I was unable to do at his age.

Life was like this, I thought to myself … a constant morphing of phenomena, both familiar and unfamiliar, into new forms. Everything was arising and passing, arising and passing. The business grew, the Trust grew, the children grew. I was a spectator, one level removed from the beating heart of these activities. I had let go of my proximity to action, loosened the tight grip we so often wield over things we call our own. Instead, I paced in the twilight, watching how life was made up of crests and lulls.

My father passed away in 2013. Even though we had known for some time that his health was failing, his death was still a mute shock to me, an event beyond my comprehension. For a long time I could not even bring myself to admit that he was gone, and I did not realize that this meant I could not properly mourn.

What I missed most about my father were his stories. His narratives of his experiences would ricochet into my consciousness during some relevant moment far later. He was a deliberate man, always teaching without posing as a teacher, always hinting without forcing. Aware that I myself was ageing and distant events would move beyond immediate recall, I looked for a way to record some of my family's stories.

Around this time I was introduced to the idea of oral history, a way of archiving the past. The idea was that while scholarship and impersonal accounts served as important records, the memories and lived experiences of individuals or communities offered precious insight into history and culture. Oral transmission of information was the oldest way that customs and histories had been transferred from one generation to the next, revealing not only the content of experiences but also the intricate workings of memory itself.

I decided to be interviewed for such an oral history, which would be stored and kept for my children. It was a way to preserve the stories that I could no longer retrieve from my father, stories about our family history that I knew would become more faint with each generation. It was also a way to give my children some understanding of their origins, to explain the principles that went into the design of their lives.

I was reminded of a saying that was carved above the door of my old school: *The axe forgets, the tree remembers.* To remember, in my mind, has always been a grave responsibility.

———

On the first day of the oral history interviews, I felt acutely nervous, as if something was having trouble settling in my stomach. I walked into the Mytrah office on High Street Kensington and almost hoped that the interviewer I was scheduled to meet would not turn up. During the course of our first meeting, I went from extreme anxiety to slowly easing into a more comfortable rhythm, aided by the interviewer's gentle prodding.

We ended up conducting six sessions that totalled to over eleven hours of interview. Starting with my grandfather's move to Tarnaka, I traced everything I could remember about my family, from my father, uncles and aunts to my children. The interviewer, Cathy, gently redirected my train of thought when it strayed, and probed for details when I was too vague or hurried.

I relived one potent memory after another. I was back in Tarnaka again, being woken up by my sister in the morning. I was throwing my bike down at the entrance of Golconda fort. I was watching my father and mother sit outside their gas station on chairs, my mother knitting something in wool, both looking as if they were on a beachside vacation as opposed to holding guard over their livelihood.

I was meeting Helen again and bringing my children home. I was drafting the 'Ten Commandments' with Vikram by my side. As I spoke, the tapestry of the past came back to me like a phantom limb, something you knew was no longer there but could suddenly feel the sensation of.

Memory is a strange thing, I thought to myself – it could awaken with a question, a song, a smell, or something as simple and inexplicable as sunlight drenching the afternoon in a particular way. After going through the oral history exercise, I discovered that life was even stranger – it was all a collection of fleeting events, splotches of colour in the mind. Although the fine grain of the story was often lost, you could trace a distinct arc by piecing together just a few key moments.

At the end of our last session, I felt a wave of exhaustion, as if all energy and emotion had been sucked out of me. Cathy's expression showed that she felt the same way.

'You're a good storyteller,' she said after a long pause. 'I'm really glad you decided to do this.'

I shook my head and laughed. 'You must think this is all very self-aggrandizing, very silly. I don't think I've ever spoken so much about myself, ever.'

'It's not going to work though, is it?'

'Is what not going to work?'

'Depending on the voluntary abdication of wealth by wealth creators. Waiting for everyone to get onboard with the trusteeship vision. It doesn't seem like that's where the world is going.'

'That's true,' I said carefully. 'There's no guarantee and not enough incentive in the world pushing people towards adopting trusteeship.'

'I still think it's an important story,' she added, sensing my slight dismay.

I was surprised at the surge of emotion in me. 'It's just ...,' I continued shakily, 'I ... I ... I want my children to understand. The normal Indian way is to give everything, including your business and your wealth, to your children. I want them to know there's an important reason why we took a different approach. Why we took such care to build something with principle, the principle that our responsibility as lucky winners in this system is to set up new rules that create value with a bigger family in mind, the family of the world. But that principle also means that my children cannot expect the same treatment from their parents as their friends do.' My voice cracked. 'I am still a human, you know. Just like any parent, I want them to have the best things. Sometimes I fear I am being unfair.'

'You are not being unfair,' Cathy said, with a look of intense concentration. 'I think it is a very noble thing you have done. And this does not only concern your family.'

'What do you mean?'

'Your life story has been an active search for understanding value, for defining what is valuable beyond what society tells you. Like you said, that does not just concern your immediate family, but a bigger family: the family of the world. This search for value is an important exercise for everyone. In fact, I would say it's your responsibility to share this story.'

'Thank you for your story, Ravi,' she said, when we stood up to leave the office. And with that, we said our goodbyes and stepped out into the cold to go our own ways.

———

The oral history process sparked another intense period of reflection in my life. As I did my customary pacing around in my apartment in London, a thought struck me repeatedly and with increasing urgency with each passing day: Was I doing enough? How was I actually creating value in the world? As an entrepreneur who was still building and growing competitive businesses that abided by all the rules of the status quo, how much impact could I have on the way the world worked?

I was not a social entrepreneur who built ventures with the explicit goal of creating a socially-minded product or service. My approach was to play by the rules of the game, to build competitive businesses in the most profitable opportunities I could find. I did not judge these opportunities by their social impact. Instead, I redistributed rewards at the last stage of the process. So, even though the profits from the businesses I built were ultimately and automatically redirected to social good, the businesses I built were indistinguishable from any other for-profit company in the world.

The cognitive dissonance that I felt after leaving Vipassana was now a constant in my life, and the two roles that I played often collided, exposing friction and contradiction: the businessman versus the social advocate, the capitalist versus the revolutionary, the man in action asserting his ego versus the detached meditator who shied away from attention. Sometimes I felt these two personalities rise up in battle within me, fighting for attention. Trying to resolve the uneasy tension between the two into some sort of equilibrium is a continual challenge, but a worthy one. It is a process that never ends, but resurfaces over and over again. I did not know if I would ever find peace.

There were days when this cognitive dissonance would harden into guilt. On those days I would think to myself that I was not someone who had presented any solution to the world, but someone who had been simply fortunate enough to be shielded from action and toil. I enjoyed a quality of life that most of my fellow brothers and sisters on Earth could never even imagine for themselves, and my ability to live in abstraction, in observation, was little more than a byproduct of no longer needing to worry about material comforts.

Yet, each time I was tempted to sink into guilt or abandon my attempt at finding a resolution between the two forces inside me, something held me back. A whisper that asked me not to give up, but to work through the contradiction and confront it, face to face.

Each of us holds some set of core beliefs about the world. Often, when we are presented with evidence that contradicts our core beliefs, we refuse to accept the new evidence, to hold the contradiction of our new realization in our mind. To avoid the discomfort of contradiction and protect our core beliefs, we choose to ignore evidence that forces us to reassess the world.

Throughout my life, I have confronted contradiction again and again, and to this day I live with the contradictions internal to my very being. But in the process I have learned that discomfort is not something to escape, but something to embrace. We all live in contradiction: as individual selves and parts of a whole, as realists and idealists, as self-interested egos and decentred minds. Working through such contradiction is not always a pleasant task. But this task of understanding and working through the relationship between our lives as individuals and our lives as a part of a greater collective of beings and meaning is an important one. It was something that, however difficult, I would not give up.

One afternoon, on an impulse, I dialled Cathy's number. She had mentioned something about moving back to New York, so I was not even sure if the number would work, but she answered immediately. She seemed pleasantly surprised to hear from me.

'I've been thinking about what you said,' I began uneasily.

Her voice, slightly broken up by static, travelled across the Atlantic. 'What did I say, exactly?'

'That it is a responsibility of mine not only to go through my personal journey and share it with my family, but to make a public stance in whatever way I can about my convictions. Especially my belief that our current way of creating value and allocating rewards in society is deeply troubling. It has been eating away at me, the suspicion that I am not doing enough. Maybe I can do more.'

'I won't have many original thoughts or solutions,' I admitted. 'but I thought you could help me.'

'That is very brave,' she said. 'I don't have much experience and I don't know what you're planning, but I'll try to help you in whatever way I can.' Even the smallest drop of suggestion in a sea of ideas, she said, could be helpful.

Over the next few months, we laid out a plan, not only to work on a set of ideas, but to also bring a group of smart young people together to brainstorm ideas alongside us. These young people came from a diverse set of academic interests and personal backgrounds. As an icebreaker, we all met in London, and spent an entire week discussing topics as wide-ranging as non-egocentric philosophies, the Scandinavian welfare system and theories of the universe. After that we spent a year putting together a large portfolio of research. And although less than 5 per cent of that effort has made it to this final manuscript, I learned more in this year than I ever thought was possible.

This book is the product of that group, and although I watched the project progress from the sidelines, they were the true engines and forgers of what you now hold in your hands.

———

I feel that my life has been an asymptotic journey from striver to witness. The striver grips tightly onto life and an idea of the self, and fights always to strengthen, to ascend, to possess. In contrast, the witness takes care not to disturb life, grazing its surface gently, and working always to detach, to observe, to examine, without making itself known.

The striver identifies with the mind and tries to enforce its wishes on the world. The witness separates and observes the mind as it observes everything else; the witness wishes to enforce nothing. The striver thinks with the 'I'. The witness does not believe the 'I' exists. The striver seeks to become the best singular self. The witness seeks the art of being among all beings.

I will never become a pure witness, since the only way to do so would be to remove myself from everything. Very few in the world have been able to do this, to give up the ego entirely and exist as a hermit or in complete service to the greater good. Yet I know that I am both striver and witness, that both exist in tension within me, and that it is my responsibility always to question and challenge the relationship between those two forces.

'Keep me fully glad with nothing,' the revolutionary poet Tagore wrote, 'Only take my hand in your hand.' In the midst of my struggle with contradiction, during what I believe to be the best and last stage of my life, this line comes back to me often, like a message in a bottle washing up on the shoreline of one's hometown. And every time, the same questions I had asked since Vipassana come back.

What did I have?

What did I need?

What did I value?

When did I offer my hand?

And the reminder: anicca, anicca, anicca.

NOTES

---························❧❦·························---

1: Descending from the Peak

1. Eisenmann, Thomas, 'Entrepreneurship: A Working Definition', *Harvard Business Review*, 10 January 2013. www.hbr.org/2013/01/what-is-entrepreneurship.

3: The Art of Tangential Solutions

1. Singh 2005 explores the growth of Foreign Direct Investment (FDI) in India from 1991 to 2005; Goldstein 2008 takes the Tatas as a case study of the internationalization of Indian companies.
2. Agar 2013 offers a global history of the mobile phone technology, and the anthropologist Tenhunen (2008) studies the impact of mobile phones on Indian villages.
3. Yoffie and Wang 2002 look at the so-called 'Cola Wars' as they progressed into the twenty-first century.

4. See 'Options Contract' 2018 for a general overview.

5: Confronting Anicca (Impermanence)

1. See Goenka 2006 at www.events.dhamma.org/presskit/2006-05/GoenkaBio.pdf
2. The descriptions of the technique itself are intentionally vague, in the interest of maintaining the integrity of the teachings for readers who are interested in attending a retreat themselves.
3. Fryba, Mirko, *Art of Happiness: Teachings of Buddhist Psychology*, Boulder, Colorado: Shambhala Publications, 1989.

6: A Changed Man

1. Hill, Nathaniel, *The Nix*, New York: Knopf, 2016.

Part 2: Myth of the Entrepreneur

1. Schweickart, Russell, 'No Frames, No Boundaries: Connecting with the whole planet - from space', *IN CONTEXT*, No. 3 Rediscovering the American Vision, Context Institute, Summer 1983.
2. See '2017 Edelman Trust Barometer.' Other surveys, like Pew Research Center, document similar trends; in their 2017 'Public Trust in Government' article, Pew reported how only 18 per cent of Americans say they trust in government as of the year in writing. For a general history, see Gordon 2012.
3. Yan, Alice, 'Rise of "entrepreneur worship" in China encourages more people to set up shop', *South China Morning Post*, 14 July 2017. http://www.scmp.com/news/china/money-wealth/article/1838562/rise-entrepreneur-worship-china-encourages-more-people-set
4. See Kenney 2000; Rao and Scaruffi 2013; Berlin 2017 for a history, development, and impact of Silicon Valley.
5. The term 'creative destruction' was coined by the Austrian-American economist Joseph Schumpeter in his 1942 magnum

opus, *Capitalism, Socialism, and Democracy*. Following Marx, Schumpeter argued that technological innovation leads to the creation of new products and services through the destruction of old industries and modes of production. To that extent, Schumpeter viewed the entrepreneur as the primary agent driving economic growth through the process of creative destruction. See Schumpeter 1942.

7: Rules and Rewards

1. For a history on the economics of hunter-gatherer societies, see Flannery and Marcus 2012; Gowdy 1997; for collective action before the rise of modern nation-states, see Blanton and Farther 2007; Boehm 2009 provides an account from a biological anthropologist perspective of the hierarchical and egalitarian forms of human organization.
2. Credit Suisse Research Institute, 'Global Wealth Report 2017', https://www.credit-suisse.com/corporate/en/research/research-institute/global-wealth-report.html.
3. Ibid.
4. Credit Suisse 2017.
5. Bricker, Jesse, Lisa J. Dettling, Alice Henriques and Joanne W. Hsu, 'Changes in US Family Finances from 2013 to 2016: Evidence from the Survey of Consumer Finances', *Federal Reserve Bulletin* 103, 2017.
6. Piketty 2014 draws on historical trends in the concentration of wealth and income from the 18th to the 20th centuries to argue that current wealth disparities have not been as entrenched and dramatic as before the First World War. His theory of capital and inequality is defined by the equation $r > g$, where r is the rate of the return to wealth and g is the rate of economic growth. Insofar as that relationship persists, wealth inequalities will continue undeterred, leading Piketty to conclude that only a global tax on wealth can reverse the current predicament. For a general overview

of income inequality in the 20th century in the United States, see Piketty and Saez 2003.

7. For the emergence of social movements contesting income inequality, see Van Gelder 2011, Gitlin 2012; Tapia *et al* 2014; Iglesias 2015; Mouffe 2016.

8. There are thinkers who have written very persuasively about how to situate these instrumental reasons in a broader framework of justice and rights ('intrinsic' goods or reasons), and although I will not touch on these topics here, I highly recommend anyone interested to look into Amartya Sen's remarkable efforts in this direction, particularly in his book *Development as Freedom*. I also recommend John Rawls's *Theory of Justice* as the pioneering text in the field of distributive justice.

9. Countries with higher inequalities have higher levels of adult obesity, mental illness, addiction to illegal drugs, and deaths from drug overdose. See Wilkinson and Pickett 2009, especially figure 5.1, figure 5.3 and figure 7.1. For an analysis of teenage pregnancies in the US, showing their prevalence in the states with the most inequality, see Ventura, Matthews, and Hamilton 2002.

10. For the effects of inequality on community values and social cohesion, see data from the European Values Study Group and World Values Survey Association 2005; in the United States, Wilkinson and Pickett 2009 use data from the National Opinion Research Center to show that states with lower levels of inequality such as North Dakota have higher levels of trust (67 per cent) than those with wide disparities in wealth like Mississippi, where only 17 per cent of the population believe that people can be trusted.

11. Wilkinson, Richard, 'Why is violence more common where inequality is greater?', *Annals of the New York Academy of Sciences*, No. 1036, 2004, pp. 1–12; Daly, Martin, Margo Wilson and Shawn Vasdev, 'Income Inequality and Homicide Rates in Canada and the United States', *Canadian Journal of Criminology*, Vol. 43, 2001, p. 219; Fajnzylber, Pablo, Daniel Lederman, and Norman Loayza,

'Inequality and Violent Crime', *The Journal of Law and Economics*, Vol. 45, No. 1, 2002, pp. 1–39.

12. Conservatives like Arthur Brooks, the president of the American Enterprise Institute, believe that social mobility and equality of opportunity are more important than economic inequality. In an interview in 2015, he said 'I don't care about income inequality per se; I care about opportunity inequality … I want everybody to have a chance to be mobile, to rise, for everybody to have a chance to earn success.' See 'Meet Arthur Brooks' 2015.

13. Corak, Miles, 'Inequality from Generation to Generation: The United States in Comparison', Graduate School of Public and International Affairs University of Ottawa, Ottawa, Canada, 2012.

14. For studies on the effects of economic inequality of political instability and unrest, see Alesina and Perotti 1996; and Keefer and Knack 2002. For the impact of inequality on social mobility, see Banerjee and Newman 1993; Owen and Weil, 1998; and Hassler *et al.*, 2007.

15. Brueckner and Lederman 2015 found that GDP per capita is reduced by 1.1 per cent over a five-year period for a 1 percentage point increase in the Gini coefficient. In addition, income inequality also affects investment and human capital. In poor countries, increase in income inequality increases the aggregate level of human capital; however, in middle-income and high-income countries, rising income inequality has a negative effect on the average years of schooling and secondary education.

16. Wilkinson and Pickett 2009 use OECD data to show that more egalitarian societies spend a higher proportion of their national income on foreign aid. The United Nations' target for foreign aid spending is 0.7 per cent of Gross National Income. Yet, on average, the countries with the least disparities in income spend four times as much as their most unequal counterparts.

17. Davis, Alyssa and Lawrence Mishel, 'CEO Pay Continues to Rise as Typical Workers are Paid Less', Economic Policy Institute, Issue Brief #380, 12 June 2014, www.epi.org/publication/ceo-pay-continues-to-rise.

18. Smith, Adam, *An Inquiry into the Nature and Causes of the Wealth of Nations*, London: W. Strahan and T. Cadell, 1776.

19. For sociological research on the effects of automation on the workplace, see Liker, Haddad, Karlin 1999; and Burris 1998. Levy and Murnane 2004 analyses the effects on the division of labour, whereas Jaimovich and Siu 2012 study the effects on job market polarization and jobless recoveries.

20. Ford, Martin, *Rise of the Robots: Technology and the Threat of a Jobless Future*, New York: Basic Books, 2016.

21. For a general overview of machine learning, big data, and artificial intelligence, see Brynjolfsson and McAffee, 2014. The science journalist Nicholas Carr has written extensively on the cognitive and social effects of automation, information technology, and the Internet. See Carr (2008, 2011, 2015).

22. Frey, Carl Benedikt and Michael A. Osborne, 'The Future of Employment: How Susceptible Are Jobs to Computerisation?', Oxford Martin School, Programme on the Impacts of Future Technology, 17 September 2013, p. 38.

23. Manyika, James, Susan Lund, Michael Chui, Jacques Bughin, Jonathan Woetzel, Parul Batra, Ryan Ko, and Saurabh Sanghvi, 'Technology, Jobs, and the Future of Work'. Briefing Note, San Francisco: McKinsey Global Institute, 2017.

9: Going Public

1. Harvey, David, *A Brief History of Neoliberalism*, Oxford: Oxford University Press, 2007, p. 39.

2. The Mont Pèlerin Society (MPS) was formed by a group of economists, historians and philosophers opposed to state intervention and any other collectivist ideologies. The members began to refer to themselves as 'neoliberals' in the 1950s. For a history of MPS, see Hartwell 1995; Mirowski 2013; and Mirowski and Plehwe 2015.

3. There were certainly other parts of the world economy that functioned differently: China's state-capitalist model, Saudi Arabia's resource-rich monarchy, or the Scandinavian welfare states, to name just a few. Yet the neoliberal 'Washington Consensus' born out of policy in the UK/US, two of the most powerful nations in the world, was the dominant ideology effecting the most global impact well into the 21st century.

4. See Chomsky 1999; Stiglitz 2002; Harvey 2007; and Steger and Roy 2010 for the history of the IMF and the World Bank and the effects of their policies on developing nations. For a philosophical exploration and critique of neoliberalism, see Foucault 2008; Brown 2015; and Leshem 2016. For anthropological research on the effects of neoliberalism on specific geographies, see Ong 2006; Comaroff and Comaroff 2001; and Ferguson (2006, 2010). Journalists like Klein 2007 and Loewenstein 2015 have examined the application of neoliberal shock doctrine after natural disasters or other historical moments of political and economic crises.

10: Trusteeship

1 Young, Michael, 'Down with Meritocracy', *The Guardian*, 29 June 2001, www.theguardian.com/politics/2001/jun/29/comment.

BIBLIOGRAPHY

———◆❋◆———

Acemoglu, Daron and James A. Robinson, 'Why Did the West Extend the Franchise? Democracy, Inequality, and Growth in Historical Perspective', *The Quarterly Journal of Economics*, Vol. 115, No. 4, 2000, pp. 1167–99.

——, *Economic Origins of Dictatorship and Democracy*, Cambridge, UK: Cambridge University Press, 2005.

Agar, Jon, *Constant Touch: A Global History of the Mobile Phone*. London: Icon Books Ltd, 2013.

Alesina, A. and R. Perotti, 'Income Distribution, Political Instability and Investment', *European Economic Review*, Vol. 40, No. 6, 1996, pp. 1203–28.

Allen, Charles, *Ashoka: The Search for India's Lost Emperor*, London: Hachette UK, 2012.

Ang, Yuen Yuen, *How China Escaped the Poverty Trap*, New York: Cornell University Press, 2016.

Ansell, David, *The Death Gap: How Inequality Kills*, Chicago: The University of Chicago Press, 2017.

Balasubramanyam, Vudayagiri N. and Vidya Mahambare, 'Foreign Direct Investment in India,' Working Paper, Lancaster University Management School, Economics Department, 2003.

Banerjee, Abhijit V. and Andrew F. Newman, 'Occupational Choice and the Process of Development', *Journal of Political Economy*, Vol.101, No. 2, 1993, pp. 274–98.

Berlin, Leslie, *Troublemakers: Silicon Valley's Coming of Age*, New York: Simon and Schuster, 2017.

Blanton, Richard and Lane Fargher, *Collective Action in the Formation of Pre-Modern States*, Berlin: Springer Science & Business Media, 2007.

Boehm, Christopher, *Hierarchy in the Forest: The Evolution of Egalitarian Behavior*, Cambridge, Massachusetts: Harvard University Press, 2001.

Boix, Carles, *Democracy and Redistribution*, Cambridge, UK: Cambridge University Press, 2003.

Bonica, Adam, Nolan McCarty, Keith T. Poole and Howard Rosenthal, 'Why Hasn't Democracy Slowed Rising Inequality?' *Journal of Economic Perspectives*, Vol. 27, No. 3, 2013, pp. 103–24.

Brandolini, Andrea, 'Political Economy and the Mechanics of Politics', *Politics & Society*, Vol. 38, No. 2, 2010, pp. 212–26.

Bricker, Jesse, Lisa J. Dettling, Alice Henriques and Joanne W. Hsu, 'Changes in US Family Finances from 2013 to 2016: Evidence from the Survey of Consumer Finances', *Federal Reserve Bulletin* 103, 2017.

Brown, Wendy, *Undoing the Demos*, Cambridge, Massachusetts: MIT Press, 2015.

Brueckner, M and D. Lederman, 'Effects of Income Inequality on Aggregate Output', World Bank Policy Discussion Paper 7317, 2015.

Brynjolfsson, Erik and Andrew McAfee, *The Second Machine Age: Work, Progress, and Prosperity in a Time of Brilliant Technologies*, New York: W.W. Norton & Company, 2014.

Buffet, Warren, 'My Philanthropic Pledge', *Fortune Magazine*, 16 June 2010, http://archive.fortune.com/2010/06/15/news/newsmakers/ Warren_Buffett_Pledge_Letter.fortune/index.htm. (Accessed on 13 February 2018).

Burris, Beverly H. 'Computerization of the Workplace', *Annual Review of Sociology*, Vol. 24, No.1, 1998, pp. 141–57.

Carland Jr, James W., Jo Ann C. Carland and James W. Trey Carland III, 'Self-actualization: The Zenith of Entrepreneurship', *Journal of Small Business Strategy*, Vol. 6, No. 1, 1995, pp. 53–66.

Carlyle, Thomas, *On Heroes, Hero-Worship and the Heroic in History*, New York: Fredrick A. Stokes & Brother, 1888.

Carr, Nicholas, *The Glass Cage: Where Automation Is Taking Us*, London: Random House, 2015.

——, *The Shallows: What the Internet Is Doing to Our Brains*, New York: W.W. Norton & Company, 2011.

——, *The Big Switch: Rewiring the World, from Edison to Google*, New York: W.W. Norton & Company, 2008.

Chakravarty, Manas, 'The Richest 1% of Indians Now Own 58.4% of the Wealth', *Livemint.com*, 24 November 2016, www.livemint.com/Money/MML9OZRwaACyEhLzUNImnO/The-richest-1-of-Indians-now-own-584-of-wealth.html. (Accessed on 23 November 2017).

Cheru, Fantu, and Cyril Obi, *The Rise of China and India in Africa: Challenges, Opportunities and Critical Interventions*, London/ Uppsala: Zed Books/Nordiska Afrikainstitutet, 2010.

Chomsky, Noam, *Profit Over People: Neoliberalism and Global Order*, New York: Seven Stories Press, 1999.

Comaroff, Jean, and John L. Comaroff (eds), *Millennial Capitalism and the Culture of Neoliberalism*, Durham, North Carolina: Duke University Press, 2001.

Corak, Miles, 'Inequality from Generation to Generation: The United States in Comparison', Graduate School of Public and International Affairs University of Ottawa, Ottawa Canada, 2012.

Cowell, Frank, *Measuring Inequality*, Oxford: Oxford University Press, 2011

Credit Suisse Research Institute, 'Global Wealth Report 2017', https://www.credit-suisse.com/corporate/en/research/research-institute/global-wealth-report.html. (Accessed on 16 November 2017).

Daly, Martin, Margo Wilson and Shawn Vasdev, 'Income Inequality and Homicide Rates in Canada and the United States', *Canadian Journal of Criminology*, Vol. 43, 2001, p. 219.

Davis, Alyssa and Lawrence Mishel, 'CEO Pay Continues to Rise as Typical Workers are Paid Less', Economic Policy Institute, Issue Brief #380, 12 June 2014, www.epi.org/publication/ceo-pay-continues-to-rise. (Accessed on 24 January 2018).

Deaton, Angus, 'Measuring Poverty in a Growing World (Or Measuring Growth in a Poor World)', *The Review of Economics and Statistics*, Vol. 87, No. 1, 2005, pp. 1–19.

Department of Telecommunications, Ministry of Communications and Information Technology, Government of India, 'New Telecom Policy', 1999, see http://www. dot. gov. in/ntp/ntpl999. htm.

Dhammika, Ven S, *The Edicts of King Asoka*, Kandy: Buddhist Publication Society, 1993.

Eisenmann, Thomas, 'Entrepreneurship: A Working Definition', *Harvard Business Review*, 10 January 2013. www.hbr.org/2013/01/what-is-entrepreneurship

European Values Study Group and World Values Survey Association, 'European and World Values Survey Integrated Data File, 1999–2001', Release 1. Ann Arbor, Michigan: Inter-university Consortium for Political and Social Research, 2005.

Fajnzylber, Pablo, Daniel Lederman, and Norman Loayza, 'Inequality and Violent Crime', *The Journal of Law and Economics*, Vol. 45, No. 1, 2002, pp. 1–39.

Ferguson, James. *Global Shadows: Africa in the Neoliberal World Order*, Durham, North Carolina: Duke University Press, 2006.

——,. 'The Uses of Neoliberalism', *Antipode*, Vol. 41, Issue s1, 2010, pp. 166–84.

Ferriss, Timothy, *The 4-Hour Work Week: Escape the 9-5, Live Anywhere and Join the New Rich*, London: Random House, 2011.

Flannery, Kent and Joyce Marcus, *The Creation of Inequality: How Our Prehistoric Ancestors Set the Stage for Monarchy, Slavery, and Empire*, Cambridge, Massachusetts: Harvard University Press, 2012.

Ford, Martin, *Rise of the Robots: Technology and the Threat of a Jobless Future*, New York: Basic Books, 2016.

Foucault, Michel, *The Birth of Biopolitics: Lectures at the Collège de France, 1978-1979*, Berlin: Springer, 2008.

Freeland, Chrystia, *Plutocrats: The Rise of the New Global Super-Rich and the Fall of Everyone Else*, London: Penguin, 2012.

Frey, Carl Benedikt and Michael A. Osborne, 'The Future of Employment: How Susceptible Are Jobs to Computerisation?', Oxford Martin School, Programme on the Impacts of Future Technology, 17 September 2013, p. 38.

Fryba, Mirko, *Art of Happiness: Teachings of Buddhist Psychology*, Boulder, Colorado: Shambhala Publications, 1989.

Gordon, Gauchat, 'Politicization of Science in the Public Sphere: A Study of Public Trust in the United States, 1974 to 2010', *American Sociological Review*, Vol. 77, No. 2, 2012, pp. 167–87.

Gitlin, Todd. *Occupy Nation: The Roots, Spirit, and the Promise of Occupy Wall Street*, New York: HarperCollins, It Books, 2012.

Goda, Thomas, 'Global trends in relative and absolute income inequality', *Ecos de Economía*, Vol. 20, No. 42, 2016, pp. 46–69.

Goenka, Satya Narayan, 'Meditation Now: Inner Peace for Inner Wisdom', www.events.dhamma.org/presskit/2006-05/GoenkaBio.pdf, 2006

Goldstein, Andrea, 'The Internationalization of Indian Companies: The Case of Tata', Working Paper, Centre for Advanced Study on India (CASI), 8 February 2008.

Gopinath, C., 'Trusteeship as a moral foundation for business', *Business and Society Review*, Vol. 110, No. 3, 2005, pp. 331–44.

Gowdy, John, *Limited Wants, Unlimited Means: A Reader on Hunter-Gatherer Economics and the Environment*, Washington, D.C: Island Press, 1997.

Guha, Ramachandra, *India After Gandhi: The History of the World's Largest Democracy*, New York: HarperCollins, Ecco, 2007.

Hardoon, Deborah, Sophia Ayele and Ricardo Fuentes-Nieva, *An Economy for the 1%*, Oxford: Oxfam International, 2016.

Hartwell, Ronald Max, *A History of the Mont Pelerin Society*, Indianapolis: Liberty Fund Inc., 1995.

Harvey, David, *A Brief History of Neoliberalism*, Oxford: Oxford University Press, 2007.

Hassler, John, José V. Rodríguez Mora and Joseph Zeira, 'Inequality and mobility', *Journal of Economic Growth*, Vol. 12, No. 3, 2007, pp. 235–59.

Hickel, Jason, 'Global Inequality May Be Much Worse Than We Think', *The Guardian*, 8 April 2016, www.theguardian.com/global-development-professionals-network/2016/apr/08/global-inequality-may-be-much-worse-than-we-think. (Accessed on 18 January 2018).

Hill, Nathaniel, *The Nix*, New York: Knopf, 2016.

Hook, Sidney, *The Hero in History: A Study in Limitation and Possibility*, New Jersey: Transaction Publishers, 1957.

Institute for Policy Studies, 'Annual CEO Compensation Survey', Washington, DC: Institute for Policy Studies, 2007.

Iglesias, Pablo, *Politics in a Time of Crisis: Podemos and the Future of Democracy in Europe*, London/New York: Verso Books, 2015.

Isaacson, Walter, *Steve Jobs*, New York: Simon Schuster, 2011.

Jaimovich, Nir and H.E. Siu, 'The Trend is the Cycle: Job Polarization and Jobless Recoveries (No. w18334)', National Bureau of Economic Research, USA, 2012.

Jain, Andrea, 'Modern Yoga', *Oxford Research Encyclopedia of Religion*, 2016.

Kapoor, Archna, *Gandhi's Trusteeship: Concept and Relevance*, New Delhi: Deep & Deep Publication, 1993.

Keefer, P. and S. Knack, 'Polarization, Politics and Property Rights: Links between Inequality and Growth', *Public Choice* 111, 2002, pp. 127–154.

Keister, Lisa. 'Meet America's Uber Wealthy "Double Rich",' Inequality. org. April 10, 2014. https://inequality.org/research/meet-americas-double-rich/. (Accessed on 16 November 2017).

Kenney, Martin. *Understanding Silicon Valley: The Anatomy of an Entrepreneurial Region*, Palo Alto: Stanford University Press, 2000.

Klein, Naomi. *The Shock Doctrine: The Rise of Disaster Capitalism*, New York: Picador, 2007.

Kochhar, Rakesh, 'A Global Middle Class Is More Promise Than Reality: From 2001 to 2011, Nearly 700 Million Step Out of Poverty, But Most Only Barely', *Pew Research Center*, 2014.

Korinek, Anton, Johan A. Mistiaen and Martin Ravallion, 'Survey nonresponse and the distribution of income', *The Journal of Economic Inequality*, Vol. 4, No. 1, 2006, pp. 33–55.

Lahiri, Nayanjot, *Ashoka in Ancient India*, Cambridge, Massachusetts: Harvard University Press, 2015.

Lakner, Christoph and Branko Milanovic, 'Global Income Distribution: From the Fall of the Berlin Wall to the Great Recession', World Bank Working Paper No. 6719, December 2013.

Lala, Russi M., *The Creation of Wealth: A Tata Story*, Bombay: IBH, 1981.

Leshem, Dotan, *The Origins of Neoliberalism: Modeling the Economy from Jesus to Foucault*, New York: Columbia University Press, 2016.

Levy, Frank and Richard J. Murnane, *The New Division of Labor: How Computers Are Creating the Next Job Market*, New Jersey: Princeton University Press, 2004.

Liker, Jeffrey K., Carol J. Haddad and Jennifer Karlin, 'Perspectives on Technology and Work Organization', *Annual Review of Sociology*, Vol. 25, No.1, 1999, pp. 575–96.

Loewenstein, Antony, *Disaster Capitalism*, London/New York: Verso Books, 2015.

Manyika, James, Susan Lund, Michael Chui, Jacques Bughin, Jonathan Woetzel, Parul Batra, Ryan Ko, and Saurabh Sanghvi, 'Technology, Jobs, and the Future of Work'. Briefing Note, San Francisco: McKinsey Global Institute, 2017.

Marmot, M.G., G. Rose, M. Shipley, and P.J. Hamilton, 'Employment grade and coronary heart disease in British civil servants', *Journal of Epidemiology and Community Health*, Vol. 32, No. 4, 1978, pp. 244–49.

'Meet Arthur Brooks, The Republican Party's Poverty Guru', NBC News.com, 13 February 2015, www.nbcnews.com/politics/politics-news/meet-arthur-brooks-republican-partys-poverty-guru-n305951. (Accessed on 23 January 2018).

Meredith, Robyn, *The Elephant and the Dragon: The Economic Rise of India and China, and What it Means for the Rest of Us*, New York: W.W. Norton & Company, 2007.

Milanovic, B., 'Globalization and inequality, Introduction to the volume of selected readings, B. Milanovic (ed.), *Globalization and inequality*,' London: Edward Elgar, 2012.

Mirowski, Philip, *Never Let a Serious Crisis Go to Waste: How Neoliberalism Survived the Financial Meltdown*, London/New York: Verso Books, 2013.

Mirowski, Philip, and Dieter Plehwe (eds), *The Road from Mont Pèlerin: The Making of the Neoliberal Thought Collective, With a New Preface*, Cambridge, Massachusetts: Harvard University Press, 2015.

Mouffe, Chantal, *Podemos: In the Name of the People*, London: Lawrence & Wishart, 2016.

Naughton, Barry, *The Chinese Economy: Transitions and Growth*, Cambridge, Massachusetts: MIT Press, 2007.

O'Clery, Cono, *The Billionaire Who Wasn't: How Chuck Feeney Secretly Made and Gave Away a Fortune*, New York: Public Affairs, 2013.

Ong, Aihwa, *Neoliberalism as Exception: Mutations in Citizenship and Sovereignty*, Durham, North Carolina: Duke University Press, 2006.

'Options Contract', Investopedia, www.investopedia.com/terms/o/optionscontract.asp. (Accessed on 16 January 2018).

Osberg, Lars and Timothy Smeeding, '"Fair" inequality? Attitudes toward pay differentials: The United States in comparative perspective', *American Sociological Review*, Vol. 71, No. 3, 2006, pp. 450–73.

Owen, Ann L. and David N. Weil, 'Intergenerational earnings mobility, inequality and growth', *Journal of Monetary Economics*, Vol. 41, No. 1, 1998, pp. 71–104.

Pew Research Center, 'Public Trust in Government: 1958–2017', 3 May 2017. http://www.people-press.org/2017/05/03/public-trust-in-government-1958-2017. (Accessed on 16 January 2018).

Piketty, Thomas, *Capital in the Twenty-first Century*, Cambridge, Massachusetts: Harvard University Press, 2014.

Piketty, Thomas, and Emmanuel Saez, 'Income inequality in the United States, 1913–1998', *The Quarterly Journal of Economics*, Vol. 118, No. 1, 2003, pp. 1–41.

Pimentel, Diego Alejo Vázquez, Iñigo Macías Aymar and Max Lawson, 'Reward Work, Not Wealth', Oxford, United Kingdom: Oxfam International, 2018.

Pizzigati, Sam, 'The "Self-Made" Hallucination of America's Rich', Institute for Policy Studies, 24 September 2012.

Polanyi, Karl, *The Great Transformation*, Boston: Beacon Press, 1944.

Rao, Arun, and Piero Scaruffi, *A History of Silicon Valley: The Largest Creation of Wealth in the History of the Planet; 1900-2013*, Palo Alto: Omniware Group, 2013.

Rao, Siriginidi Subba, 'Bridging digital divide: Efforts in India', *Telematics and Informatics*, Vol. 22, No. 4, 2005, pp. 361–75.

Rawls, John, *A Theory of Justice*, Cambridge, Massachusetts: Harvard University Press, 1971.

Rolnick, Phyllis J., 'Charity, trusteeship, and social change in India: A study of a political ideology', *World Politics*, Vol. 14, No. 3, 1962, pp. 439–60.

Rowlatt, Justin, 'Thomas Piketty: "Indian Inequality Still Hidden"', BBC News, 2 May 2016 http://www.bbc.com/news/world-asia-india-36186116. (Accessed on 23 November 2017).

Rukmini, S., 'India's Staggering Wealth Gap in Five Charts', *The Hindu*, 23 September 2017, www.thehindu.com/data/indias-staggering-wealth-gap-in-five-charts/article10935670.ece. (Accessed on 23 November 2017).

Scheidel, Walter, *The Great Leveler: Violence and the History of Inequality From the Stone Age to the Twenty-first Century'*, New Jersey: Princeton University Press, 2017.

Scheve, Kenneth and David Stasavage, 'Wealth Inequality and Democracy', *Annual Review of Political Science*, Vol. 20, No. 1, 2017, pp. 451–68.

Schiraldi, Vincent and Jason Ziedenberg, 'Cellblocks or Classrooms?: The Funding of Higher Education and Corrections and Its Impact on African-American Men', Justice Policy Institute, 2002.

Schumpeter, Joseph A., *Capitalism, Socialism and Democracy*, London: Routledge, 1942, 2013 rpt.

Schweickart, Russell, 'No Frames, No Boundaries: Connecting with the whole planet - from space', *IN CONTEXT*, No. 3 Rediscovering the American Vision, Context Institute, Summer 1983.

Sen, Amartya, *Development as Freedom*, New York: Oxford University Press, 1999.

Singh, Kulwindar, 'Foreign direct investment in India: A critical Analysis of FDI from 1991-2005,' 2005, https://papers.ssrn.com/sol3/papers.cfm?abstract_id=822584.

Smith, Adam, *An Inquiry into the Nature and Causes of the Wealth of Nations*, London: W. Strahan and T. Cadell, 1776.

Soergel, Andrew, 'World's Super Wealthy to Transfer $16 Trillion in Inheritance Over Next 30 Years', *U.S. News and World Report*, 14 January 2015.

Spencer, Herbert, *The Study of Sociology*, New York: Appleton, 1896.

Steger, Manfred B. and Ravi K. Roy. *Neoliberalism: A Very Short Introduction*, Oxford: Oxford University Press, 2010.

Stiglitz, Joseph, *Globalization and its Discontents*, New York: W.W. Norton and Company, 2002.

Tapia, Maite, Lowell Turner, and Lee H. Adle, *Mobilizing against Inequality: Unions, Immigrant Workers, and the Crisis of Capitalism*, New York: Cornell University Press, 2014

Taylor, Fiona C., Ambika Satija, Swati Khurana, Gurpreet Singh and Shah Ebrahim, 'Pepsi and Coca Cola in Delhi, India: availability, price and sales', *Public Health Nutrition*, Vol. 14, No. 4, 2011, pp. 653–60.

Tenhunen, Sirpa, 'Mobile technology in the village: ICTs, culture, and social logistics in India', *Journal of the Royal Anthropological Institute*, Vol. 14, No. 3, 2008, pp. 515–34.

Thompson, Edward P., 'History from Below', *Times Literary Supplement*, Vol. 7, No. 4, 1966, pp. 279–80.

Thussu, Daya Kishan, 'Privatizing the airwaves: The impact of globalization on broadcasting in India', *Media, Culture & Society*, Vol. 21, No. 1, 1999, pp. 125–31.

Van Gelder, Sarah (ed.), *This changes everything: Occupy Wall Street and the 99% movement*, Oakland, CA: Berrett-Koehler Publishers, 2011.

Ventura, S. J., T.J. Matthews and B.E. Hamilton, 'Teenage births in the United States: Trends, 1991–2000, an update', *National Vital Statistics Reports*, Vol. 50, No. 9, 2002.

Wilkinson, Richard, 'Why is violence more common where inequality is greater?', *Annals of the New York Academy of Sciences* No. 1036, 2004, pp. 1–12.

Wilkinson, Richard and Kate Pickett, 'Income inequality and population health: A review and explanation of the evidence', *Social Science and Medicine*, Vol. 62, No. 7, 2006, pp. 1768–84.

——, *The Spirit Level: Why Greater Equality Makes Societies Stronger*, Bloomsbury, London: Bloomsbury Press, 2009.

'World Ultra Wealth Report 2017', Wealth-X. Singapore: Wealth-X PTE-LTD, 2017.

Woods, Frederick Adams, *The Influence of Monarchs: Steps in a New Science of History*, London: Macmillan, 1913.

Woodward, David, 'Incrementum ad absurdum: global growth, inequality and poverty eradication in a carbon-constrained world', *World Economic Review* 4, 2015, pp. 43–62.

Yan, Alice, 'Rise of "entrepreneur worship" in China encourages more people to set up shop', *South China Morning Post*, 14 July 2017, http://www.scmp.com/news/china/money-wealth/article/1838562/rise-entrepreneur-worship-china-encourages-more-people-set

Yoffie, David B., and Yusi Wang, 'Cola wars continue: Coke and Pepsi in the twenty-first century', Harvard Business School Case 702–442, January 2002.

Young, Michael, 'Down with Meritocracy', *The Guardian*, 29 June 2001, www.theguardian.com/politics/2001/jun/29/comment. (Accessed on 18 January 2018).

Zinn, Howard, *A People's History of the United States*, New York: Harper & Row, 1980.

'2017 Edelman Trust Barometer', *Edelman*. 15 January 2017, www.edelman.com/executive-summary. (Accessed on 24 January 2018).

INDEX

———— ❖ ————

ABOUT THE AUTHORS

———❈———

Ravi Kailas is a serial entrepreneur who has built and scaled ventures spanning telecom, software, financial options, infrastructure and more. He currently serves as the chairman of the board of Mytrah Group, which tackles next-generation opportunities such as renewable energy, electric vehicles and deep tech in India. He spends much of his remaining time on Pravaha Trust, an open philanthropic foundation seeking to redefine development in India.

Cathy Guo is still defining her identity. She graduated from Columbia University with a degree in Economics and Philosophy. As a writer, she has primarily published poetry and (unreadable) literary theory. She now lives in Bengaluru, India, and is always looking for new stories to tell. This is her first book.